Intentional: Developing A Plan for Success for Your Small Group

JOHN M. MOZINGO

DEDICATION

To the members of every small group that I have
been a part of over the years. It was among
these amazing people that I learned to love
the way Jesus loves.

CONTENTS

ACKNOWLEDGMENTS

"Coming together is a beginning. Keeping together is progress. Working together is success." --Henry Ford.

When I started writing this book, it was purely by accident. I was simply writing some thoughts to share with my group leaders at Park Valley Church. One thought lead to many. I continued writing page after page soon realizing this was far too large for the original email post that I was working on. I soon began thinking that what I started might prove helpful to other group leaders outside the four walls of our church. I decided to write the book.

Almost immediately, I began to doubt myself. Who am I to think someone is interested in what I have to say about small groups. I suppose that is yet to be known. But God knows when we need to be encouraged and, though he could encourage us through angelic encounters or miraculous circumstances, he has chosen to use the people of his church to be our source of encouragement.

It was the encouragement from my wife and children that gave me courage to decide to create the book. I am so grateful for the family God has given me. I would be lost and without purpose if it were not for them. Thank you Melinda, Haylee, Colton, Jacob, Chloe, and Travis.

It was the people of my small group that gave me confidence to continue. Appropriately, much of the spiritual encouragement I needed came from small group studies we did and the conversations that they invoked. I am grateful to this group of people whose wise counsel I have come to depend on.

I am grateful for the handful of pastors that knew that I was writing this book. Their occasional, "how's the book coming?" or what are "you waiting for?" was enough to reset my determination and encourage me to finish. Thank you Tom, Barry, Mark, David, and Steve.

I am particularly grateful to churches that would allow me to learn from many mistakes over the years, to experience victory, and to implement the ideas that I have learned from many great men and years of ministry

Though there was never a team meeting to plan or write this book, it was most definitely a team effort. For that I am truly grateful.

INTENTIONAL

INTRODUCTION

Intentional: Developing A Plan for Success for Your Small Group

You were born to do this. Whoever you are, you were created to be a part of something intimate yet larger than yourself. We all crave it on some level. Those that isolate themselves do so because they were hurt by it. We were created to be a part of a community. This was an enormous part of God's plan for the church. Over time, we have made it complicated. The idea that we are to live, love, grow, and encourage others to do the same is foundational to God's plan for us to become more like Jesus.

The world, in its own, way recognizes this. Social media attempts to build community through the use of apps and posts and pictures. Facebook's goal is to connect the world. In his letter to the Facebook community on February 16, 2017, Mark Zuckerberg posed five questions that described Facebook's plan to build community. (Zuckerberg, 2017) Ironically, he looked to the church as an example of building a community that successfully groups people according to "interest, affinity, and aspirations." (Metz, 2017) Billions of people subscribe to Facebook and spend as much as an hour a day scrolling through others' lives. Not because we benefit from it or find anything interesting. It is instinctive. We were born for community.

If we were born for this and it is part of God's plan, why then is it often the most difficult part of ministry. Why do less than 35% of believers join a small group? Why has Sunday school attendance declined by more than 40% in less than a decade? If there were a simple answer, there would be a simple solution. The reasons are many.

It is safe to assume that you, the reader, are a small group leader. If not, you are probably a close relative of mine. Why else would anyone read this book on small group success. As the leader of your group, you are not burdened with the downward trends in discipleship in the United States. You are, however, tasked with making your group a place where people feel safe, loved, and confident that they can grow to be more like Jesus. You are not responsible for the transformations that take place in people's lives. That is still the task of the Holy Spirit and the power of God's word. Your job is to create a place where transformation can take place. To create, one must be intentional.

Being intentional and having a plan does not need to be complicated. A simple effort to make every group experience purposeful will have an enormous impact on group participation, commitment, and growth. In this book, I will encourage you to do three things that will help you to create this kind of small group experience:

1. Be intentional with every aspect of group life, not just the Bible study element. Be intentional when it comes to being social, being evangelistic, and being servants.

2. Create a year-long, flexible plan that gives purpose to every week of the year, even the weeks you may not meet.

3. Be intentional to develop a plan for each meeting that not only creates a sense of structure to your meetings but also offers the freedom and flexibility to respond to the leading of the Holy Spirit.

As you read, I encourage you to evaluate yourself and your group experience. Bring group members in on the discussion. There are real advantages to implementing a collaborative effort to adding purpose to each element of your small group.

JOHN M. MOZINGO

1 YOU NEED A PLAN

*The heart of man plans his way, but
the LORD establishes his steps.
Proverbs 16:9*

I love the day trip—taking a day off work, driving to someplace you've never been, and experiencing what the locals have to offer. When it's done, you make the short trip home and sleep in your own bed. I like that part. Hotels are expensive and generally disgusting—at least the ones I can afford. There are two ways to take the day trip—with a plan or without a plan. I've done both. I only recommend one.

One memorable day trip took place twenty-five years ago. My wife, Melinda, and I had been married only a few months. We were living in a small apartment in Jupiter, Florida. We were teachers so we had our summers free. On a whim, we took a day trip. Our destination was Lake Okeechobee. It was less than an hour away. Neither of us had ever been there. We were guided by a sense of spontaneity that we have not experienced since having children. We said let's go, got off the couch, put on our flip-flops and off we went.

On our way we talked about what we would do—rent a pontoon boat, sample the local restaurants, maybe buy some cheap fishing poles and toss a line in the water. Maybe we could stay late enough to watch the sunset beyond the western shore of the lake. One of the first things we learned about Lake Okeechobee is that it is surrounded by a man-made dike built by the Army Corps of Engineers in the 1930's. Without knowing exactly where to go, we could not even see the lake. We drove and drove. We were driving counter-clockwise around the lake, so I assumed that if I kept making left turns we would be ok. Not so. We took wrong turn after wrong turn. It was blistering hot. My Mazda 323 had no air conditioning. Central Florida is flat. One cow pasture looked exactly like the next. We discovered a Seminole Indian Reservation. Hallelujah! Something to do. We drove and drove on the reservation until we finally came to the visitor center. We went in. There was one person inside. At the risk of sounding politically incorrect, she did not look much like an Indian. As I recall, she was blonde and wearing a Budweiser T-shirt. We glanced around at the gifts in the gift shop. I picked up what appeared to be a peace pipe—again, my apologies. On the bottom, it said made in Taiwan. I put it down. We left.

After five hours of driving, we finally reached a little park on the southwest side of the lake where we could see a small—very small—lagoon-like portion that opened up to the lake in the distance. By this time, we couldn't care less. We got in the car and made the three-hour trip home. Our only stop was Burger King, which, go figure, was exactly like the Burger King that was a mile from our apartment.

I do NOT recommend this as a pleasant day trip.

Our most recent and my new favorite day trip happened just weeks ago. We now live in Northern Virginia. For Melinda's birthday, I planned a day trip to Richmond, the state capital. I spent time online, a luxury I did not have twenty-five years and five kids ago, researching things to do, places to visit, and the best restaurants. I took into consideration the things I knew my wife liked to do. The end result was a day trip that we will never forget. We started with a 2 ½ hour bike tour around Church Hill. The tour included stops at historic places such as St. John's Church where Patrick Henry made his famous "Give me liberty or give me death," speech. It also featured stops at local eateries including a wood-fire oven bakery and a fine chocolate shop—Melinda's favorite part of the tour. We then went to the Riverfront and walked around, taking in the sites and enjoying an incredibly beautiful day. We ate at a great restaurant downtown that was in an old drug store. The food was spectacular. We ended the day by going to the Sandi Patty Farewell Tour—a favorite of ours from back in the day.

The major difference between the two day trips is the simple fact that I planned the trip to Richmond. Yes, there are times when spontaneity pays off. I love the sense of adventure. But few good things happen by accident. We most often associate the word accident with unpleasant things—spilled milk, car wrecks, and diapers. The same is true when it comes to your small group—very few good things happen by accident. Like the day trip, planning ahead can make the small group experience pleasant, fun, and meaningful.

The purpose of this book is to encourage you to think of planning in broader terms. When I was a school teacher, we referred to this as the scope and sequence. I never knew exactly what that meant, but it always ended in my making a long-term plan and setting goals for my classes. I'm not much for paperwork but I learned to value and depend on this set of plans and goals.

The same is true for your small group. Nearly everything negative associated with small groups can be avoided or work to your advantage when properly planned. But before we dig into "the plan" let me consider some thoughts about planning in general.

Planning does not mean you are ignoring the Holy Spirit.

Many people assume that making a plan, especially a plan made way in advance ignores the leading of the Holy Spirit. I could not disagree more. This assumes that the Holy Spirit is incapable of leading someone through the planning process. Some people are wired to go through life without a plan and they are happy and fulfilled to do so. But when that person is in a position of leadership, not everyone he is leading has the same carefree outlook on life. As leaders, we lead people that are confused, hurting, seeking, recovering, and more. In short, we lead people that may depend on a plan to get through the day. They find their security in the plan. The plan gives them something to look forward to. Group life characterized by a plan is more appealing and more rewarding to most people. Except for a few special people, we are wired to respond to a plan. We are created in God's image. God has a plan for mankind (Jeremiah 29:11), a plan for our redemption (Romans 10:9), a plan for our ministry (Ephesians 2:10) and the list of plans goes on. If God is the author of the ultimate plan, then certainly he created us to respond to planning.

Planning Requires Flexibility.

The Apostle Paul had a plan. His plan basically had three parts: Share the Gospel in places where there was no church; fellowship with the church in Rome; take the gospel as far away as Spain. Paul was committed to his plan but remained flexible enough to alter that plan as God brought new opportunities his way. He told the Roman church in Romans 1:13,

> *"I planned many times to visit you, but I was prevented until now."*

Paul never made it to Spain. He tried several times to get to Rome, but the needs of others, persecution, and more prevented him from going. Though his plan did not come to fruition, God had another plan that took Paul to Rome. Paul is arrested in Jerusalem in Acts 21. He pleads his case, shares his testimony, and proclaims the risen Savior any chance he can. Then in Acts 23:11, Jesus appears to Paul in prison. I love this moment. In my mind, it is one of the most intimate moments in the New Testament. The first missionary, determined to share the Gospel in Rome, sits helplessly in chains.

It's dark. Not dark like we know today. Dungeon dark. Cold air and foul smells. I can imagine the author of the words *"rejoice in the Lord, always"* being anything but joyful—discouraged more likely.

Then:

That night the Lord appeared to Paul and said, "Be encouraged, Paul. Just as you have been a witness to me here in Jerusalem, you must preach the Good News in Rome as well.

Yes. Discouraged. Jesus told him to "be encouraged," so absolutely, Paul was discouraged. I wish there were more detail. The bright light. Angels singing. Paul's face aglow like Moses' after seeing the Creator and Savior. But the description is simple. God showed up. Paul was flexible. At perhaps his darkest moment, Jesus reassures him, "this is part of the plan."

By all means, plan. The members of your group will respond to a good plan. But never be inflexible or rigid when it comes to the plan. God may show up. We can be so focused on the plan that we miss God's presence.

Be Flexible With People.

I love all the members of every small group I have ever been a part of. I've had the privilege of doing life with some truly amazing people of faith. But the first actual small group that I organized and participated in holds a special place in my heart.

I spent many years in South Florida as a teacher and

eventually a pastor. One of my responsibilities as an associate pastor of a fifty year old, well-established church was to move them from the old Sunday school model to a small group model. I had heard all the horror stories. Church splits, angry teachers, etc. But God blessed this move and with the exception of a couple glitches, the transition was great. In making this transition, I had determined to develop a model small group that others could look at and get inspiration. It would be the textbook group of like-minded, passionate Jesus followers that would charge the gates of hell with a Super Soaker and inspire a generation of people to fall in line in the newly formed army of small groups. With Melinda's help and a partnership with a few close friends, we hand-selected people that fit our demographic—late thirties to early forties with children that were eight to fifteen years old. Our plan was flawless. Our group was well-crafted. We could not lose.

God had other plans. I'm also quite sure he got a good chuckle at our efforts. We published our group in the list of newly formed small groups. "Young Families with School-aged Children. Childcare provided". How could we miss? We even had free childcare.

The group met in a room near the fellowship hall. Strategically placed signs directed people to our group. There were three couples, cut from the same mold, ready to meet the newest members of our perfect group. First to walk in was a couple that we all knew and loved. Kirk was a deacon and Clarene taught most of our kids in the three-year-old Sunday school room. In fact, Clarene had taught three-year-old Sunday school since the 70's when most of us were three years old. Clearly, they did not fit the demographic. Perhaps they read the catalog incorrectly.

Then, the parade of misfits began. A forty-year-old single mom and her twenty-year-old daughter who was also a single mom. She even brought the baby. A fifty-something-year-old lady who was recently divorced. A 35 year old man that had just completed a yearlong residential drug addiction program who was also struggling with the early stages of throat cancer. A 65 year old homeless man that lived in a van down by the river (I wish that were a joke) with a fifteen-year-old dog that he had rescued from a crack house. Yes, he brought the dog.

In fact, the only forty-ish couple with school-aged children was a homeless couple whose kids were living in a foster home in Atlanta.

What had gone wrong? We had the perfect plan. What would we do? After the first meeting, we talked. Someone suggested we just go with it. It was probably Dawn who suggested it. She loves everybody.

So we went with it. It was awkward. It was a little weird. I grew up in a sterile, Baptist environment. Here I was sitting with people that lived on the streets and smelled of alcohol and cigarettes—people characterized by breaking the commandments that were hammered into my brain since birth. Most of these people would have been shunned in the church where I grew up.

In time, it became beautiful. I learned more about people in those three years than any other time in my life. I learned what it looked like to love like Jesus loved. I saw the body of Christ, broken and flawed as it was, come together to support each other out of love.

The three original couples, who thought we had it all together, learned to rely on the wisdom of Kirk's and Clarene's experience as parents. We gave the single mom a minivan and helped her with her two special needs children. We helped the homeless man pay off his van and eventually move on to a houseboat. While the man with cancer was on the brink of death, we prayed over him and saw a miraculous healing. We helped the homeless wife get into a treatment center and eventually reunite with her children. We provided friendship to the divorced lady that was new to the area and very lonely. We prayed together through job changes and the loss of family members. Simply put, we did life together.

I can't imagine the God moments we all would have missed had we gone back to the drawing board to make our group look more like our original plan. I have eternal friendships from this group. Paul, the formerly homeless man, texts me nearly every day to tell me what God is teaching him. Almost without fail, he says just what I need to hear. My life is better for having been in a small group with what I thought was a parade of misfits. Turns out, I was the odd man out.

Be Flexible With Your Schedule.

When Melinda and I spent the day in Richmond, I had every second planned. Nothing was left to chance. However, Catherine, the bicycle tour guide, made some suggestions of things we should see. My first inclination was, "bump that, we already have a plan." But, she knew the area better. I knew nothing. She has visited these places. I had not. So, with a few minor adjustments—dinner thirty minutes later, arrive at the concert thirty minutes early instead of an hour early— we could make it to Catherine's suggested sites and still do everything else.

We were not disappointed. If you are ever in Richmond, Virginia, I recommend Maymont Gardens and the Hollywood Cemetery. Richmond Rides is the name of the bicycle tour company. You're welcome.

Had I remained inflexible I would have missed some beautiful and memorable moments. The same is true in your small group. If you are inflexible, you may miss the beautiful moments where God works in the lives of your group members. When God does something amazing in your group, it needs to be celebrated. When people are hurting, they need to be lifted up. These are the memorable moments in small group. This is where life change takes place. The chapter you have scheduled for this week can wait.

Be Flexible With Content.

If you have not already learned this, you will experience this truth at some point as a small group leader. Here it is: Just because it was published, doesn't mean it's good. No, I'm not going to tell you which ones.

There may be times when you are ten minutes into a new study and realize that it doesn't work for this particular group. My experience says to bail. If your group is obviously not clicking with the study, talk about it. They may all be feeling the same way. I think it is better to waste the $7.49 per participant book than it is to waste eight weeks of their lives. Be flexible. Cut your losses and move on to the next study.

Also, be flexible when it comes to choosing the study—you may need to do a study or two that you would rather not. You may have led it before many times. If your group needs it, go for it. It won't kill you.

The plan is good and arguably necessary for the health and success of your group. My intention is to discuss this in detail throughout this book. But for now, the best point I can make is to be flexible.

2 YOUR GROUP MEMBERS NEED YOUR PLAN

Someone is sitting in the shade today because someone planted a tree a long time ago.
-Warren Buffet

There are two questions that are most often asked in a small group. Who's bringing the food? And what are we studying next? Ok, the first one is often asked in my small group and I'm usually the one asking it. But the second question is asked frequently in all groups. It is the number one question that I am asked by leaders. It is also a very important question because your choice of study can make or break your group. If someone does not like the next topic, they may find an excuse to be somewhere else on group night. Groups also lose momentum while trying to choose the next course of study.

The scenario looks like this—your group is one week away from finishing the current study and you have no idea what to do next. There is no reason not to know, you just haven't considered it until now. "Be democratic," you tell yourself. "That's the answer."

So you throw out the question: "I was thinking about what we should study next. Does anyone have any suggestions?" There is a long, uncomfortable pause which quickly turns into a maddening silence. The feeling of Déjà vu reminds you that this happened the last time you asked this question. A sense of panic sets in just before the hush is broken by one person who can no longer stand the silence.

"I heard of a study by (insert your favorite author here). Maybe we should do that."

The suggestion hangs there for a moment like a piece of bad fruit. Because no one wants to offend the person making the suggestion, everyone agrees. Even though they are in agreement, many are thinking

> *I never liked that author.*
> *I did that study in my last group.*
> *That subject does not help me in my current situation.*
> *Who made this cheese ball? It's spectacular!*

That scenario has the potential of repeating itself over and over again every time you are in need of a new course of study for your group.

People Want To Be Led

Imagine if your pastor took the same approach on Sunday mornings. As he is wrapping up his most recent sermon series, he looks at the congregation and asks, "Ok, what shall we do next?"

A statement like this from a man called to prepare a body of believers to glorify God and point people to Jesus suggests several things. It would be a reasonable assumption that the Holy Spirit is not leading him or that he does not understand the responsibilities associated with his position. Others may assume that he is incompetent. Whatever they think, it boils down to a lack of confidence in the pastor.

Conversely, the pastor that steps on to the stage and clearly communicates a plan that engages people in the study of the Bible, the work of the ministry, and relationships with other people will generally have the confidence of the people in his church. In an article for Churchleader.com, Perry Noble lists 10 Characteristics of Growing Churches. Number one on his list is, "They have leaders that lead." (Noble, 2011) The same is true in your group. People want to be led. Don't be afraid to lead your group by developing a plan.

People Like To Know Where They Are Going

The "what shall we do next" approach to leading your group can also leave your group feeling as though they lack purpose and direction. They don't know where they are headed. They have nothing to look forward to. They may even begin thinking, "This would be a good time to make an exit." A clearly defined plan can steer your group toward confidence, purpose, and direction.

Let me describe an alternate scenario. It is late November. You are about to wrap up your most recent study. Experience tells you that December is not the best time to start a new group study unless it is short and Christmas themed. So you have opted to host a small group Christmas party complete with traditional Christmas food, ugly sweaters, and a $5 gift exchange. Your group will also serve together at your church's annual Christmas outreach event. You will take some time to relax and then regroup for the second week of January. You do the math. That's about two months before your next study will begin. Motivated by a sense of calm and confidence, you say, "I'm thinking about some different topics that we might study after the first of the year. What kind of things would you like to talk about?" The question is intentionally vague and open-ended. There is no awkward pause. The answers come quickly because they already know what they need the most—they deal with it every day so it is on the tip of their tongue.

We need help with our kids
Let's do something on marriage
What if we just take a book of the Bible and dig in
I have lots of questions about the end of the world
I'd like to know more about what the Bible says about money

The list is potentially endless. Unlike the first scenario, the answers tell you more than a list of favorite teachers and best-selling authors. It tells you what your group members are passionate about. It tells you where they need encouragement and where they are struggling. It also provides you with the framework for a long-range plan that meets the needs of your group members and gives them a sense of validation because you are intentionally including them in the process. No one is worried about hurting anyone's feelings. Everyone has something to look forward to. You are not stressed by a never-ending burden to choose the next study. Everybody wins!

People Want And Need Relationships

Let's face it. The modern American church has no lack of resources when it comes to good preaching and teaching. It is everywhere. Much of it is free and can be accessed while sitting in your pajamas with a cold slice of last night's pizza and your third cup of coffee. There are even small group studies on Netflix. So when someone starts looking for a group, they are not looking for preaching and teaching. They are looking for friends. They need people in their life that have walked a similar path. I don't mean to sound anti-Bible study. I've been accused of that before. I'm just sharing what I know to be true after many years in the trenches. I am absolutely pro-Bible study, but the reality is that people are starved for meaningful relationships.

I believe with all that is in me that life change happens in the context of relationships. I should cite a source here, but I have no idea who said this first. Kudos, whoever you are. Nevertheless, it is true and Biblical. James 5:16 is a wonderful demonstration of this.

Confess your sins to each other and pray for each other so that you may be healed. The earnest prayer of a righteous person has great power and produces wonderful results.

I'm no Greek scholar, but I assume that the folks at blueletterbible.com are. Their definition of sin or fault as it says in the KJV is a lapse or deviation from truth and uprightness. It describes sin in its broadest sense. Not only does it refer to the sinful offense, but also its consequences and the pain it causes. And the remedy is to talk about it with others. If you want healing, bring your issues into the light so that others can pray with you. If you're like most people, talking about your problems is not something you will do with just anyone. Most people will only share their shortcomings with someone to whom they are close—a friend, a relative—a relationship. In short, healthy relationships encourage life change—especially healthy relationships with Jesus at the center.

When the church where I served in Florida made the transition to a small group model, our resident counselor said something to me that I will never forget. He said that since we had made the switch to small groups, he did not have as many counseling appointments. In recent years, I have done a lot of marriage counseling. I have noticed that I rarely counsel a couple that is involved in a small group. When I do counsel people involved in a group, I encourage them to share their struggle with the members of the group. In short time, they stop coming to counseling. It's good that my counseling services are free. I would be moving in with my friend on the boat if I depended on counseling for my income.

Inevitably when someone shares their struggle in a group, they find that someone else in the group has had the same struggle or is going through it at the same time. 2 Corinthians 1:4 says,

> *He comforts us in all our troubles so that we can*
> *comfort others. When they are troubled, we will*
> *be able to give them the same comfort*
> *God has given us.*

When the relationships in your group encourage this kind of openness, God shows up and lives are changed.   Meeting the need for relationships is Biblical and healthy for your group and the individual.   Therefore, we have a responsibility to facilitate the potential for friendship as much as facilitating a Bible study. We can do this as part of the plan for our groups.   Be intentional about scheduling time to be social and time to celebrate. Your group will be forever grateful.

People Need To Serve

Jesus was a servant. He came to serve and not be served (Matthew 20:28).   Therefore, we cannot become more like Jesus apart from serving. This is discipleship at its core—leading others to become more like Jesus. As a small group leader, you play an enormous role in the discipleship of people in your group.   Not simply because you lead Bible studies, but because you are in a position to encourage people to act, think, talk, and love like Jesus. Including service and ministry in your group's plan will bring a spark of life to your group and create opportunities to be Jesus to others.   If done intentionally, it will give them the opportunity to serve according to the way God created them.

3 CREATING A YEAR LONG PLAN FOR YOUR GROUP

If you don't know where you are going,
you'll end up someplace else. -Yogi Berra

My dad will always be my greatest hero. He was a strong, quiet, godly man of integrity. I never heard him swear or a say a cross word about anyone. When he passed at 85, people came to me at his funeral telling me about his generosity and acts of kindness. I was unaware of most of them until that moment but was not at all surprised.

Dad built houses for the better part of his adult life. By building, I don't mean that he had a company that employed others to do the work of building homes. He was the owner, general contractor, supervisor, laborer, accountant—everything.   I worked with Dad during the summers. I learned more from him about hard work, honesty and integrity than I would in a lifetime of Sunday school classes.

Dad's greatest gift as a businessman was that he knew how to work and plan efficiently. He would plan way ahead. I never had the chance to talk specifically about how he did it, but it was obvious that he had an intentional plan for at least an entire year. As soon as the winter weather disappeared Dad would begin new construction, knowing that he had limited time before cold weather would return. He paced the work so that money was always available and expenses did not all hit at once. He would have two or three homes under construction at one time. Progress was intentionally paced so that he could give each new home the attention it required, hire sub-contractors and schedule inspections efficiently. When cold weather finally returned, Dad had two or three homes under roof. Even in foul weather, he could wrap up the interior construction and put on the finishing touches. Final inspections were made, contracts were signed, and the whole process started over again. While many in construction were taking time off or working in another field during winter months, Dad was still hard at work. It was never easy work, but deliberately planning out the year made his job easier, more predictable, and more profitable.

As small group leaders, we don't often think past the end of the current study. But planning ahead, as we discussed, is a win for you and your group members. Less stress, no awkward moments, and everyone has something to look forward to.

Planning out a year is relatively simple. It can be done in just a few short hours over a period of two or three days at most. Always being on the lookout for new material and opportunities will shorten the process. This kind of planning also presents opportunities to bring other group members into the process. Every group I've ever been in seems to have someone that geeks out over making spreadsheets. They are very detail oriented. If you have that person in your group, they would be a huge help to you and would appreciate your asking them to help.

Create A Group Calendar

Step one is to assemble a calendar that designates the days that you will potentially meet. I include all fifty-two of those days, even if you know you will not meet. You need to communicate that to your group also. You can do this however you like, keeping in mind that the final product needs to be something understandable that you can distribute to your group. At this stage, anything from the Calvin and Hobbs calendar you got at the small group Christmas party (maybe it's time to up the gift exchange limit to $10) to an Excel spreadsheet will do. I go with the spreadsheet. I like to see everything on one page.

If your group meets every other week or monthly, you can plug the dates in accordingly. However, let me take this time to encourage you to move to a weekly meeting schedule. Though I offer no statistical, Barna-like evidence to support this, it is my experience that groups that meet weekly form relationships faster and deeper, and they stay together longer. A single interruption in the schedule for a group that meets weekly is remedied the next week. If there is a single interruption to the schedule of a group that meets every other week, those group members may not see each other for nearly a month. I am a huge fan of weekly meetings. If your group does not meet weekly, make the move to a weekly schedule as soon as possible. You won't regret it.

Add Holidays

Next, go through and mark any holidays that will take place on or near your scheduled meeting time. Obviously, if your group is meeting the same day as Easter or Christmas, you are probably not going to meet and that should be noted on the calendar. Other holidays may indicate a three day weekend, family events, etc. that may change your normal routine. It may also present opportunities for your group to spend time together. Our current group has met for a cookout on Memorial Day for a couple years now. We all look forward to it. Now is the time to put similar opportunities on the calendar.

Add Your Church's Big Days

Next, you want to put your church's big days on the calendar. This is very important. It is vital for your group to feel connected to your church. Small groups should never encourage a sense of isolation. Being part of the church is a global experience and group leaders should intentionally keep the group connected to the mother ship. The easiest way to accomplish this is by participating as a group at your church's big days. Serve together at an outreach event, attend special services together. Support the mission and vision of your church as a group.

Add Your Church's Group Schedule

If the small group ministry of your church designates periods of time specifically for groups, include that schedule on the calendar. Your church leadership does this for a good reason. Sometimes it seems of no consequence to a group to set its own schedule but if your church has designated times, groups should recognize them. These obvious beginnings to a new small group semester, or quarter or whatever your church calls them, serve as a great on-ramp for new attendees. When everyone is on the same schedule the church can promote the small group ministry as a whole and direct people to multiple options. Groups not on the church schedule will find it difficult to welcome new people because they are in the middle of a study when new people join—very awkward timing for a newbie.

The church schedule also creates an easy exit from a group. Not everyone is a perfect fit for any group. I once spoke to a couple that was in their mid-twenties, newly married, and new attendees at their church. They were directed to a particular small group because it was close to their home. They signed up online and got an email from the group leader welcoming them to the group. They were excited to attend their first meeting. When they arrived they learned that, not only were they the youngest couple there, they were the only ones under fifty years old. Most of the group members were grandparents and near retirement age. Though there is something to be said of the benefits of wisdom from older generations, this was not what this couple needed in this season of life. They were newly married, new to the church and looking for close friendships—people that will walk the same path with them. They stuck it out for a period of time, learned from this group of wise, godly believers, and developed some good friendships. When that small group semester was over, there was an obvious time that they could make an exit without feeling awkward. The rest of the group understood and, quite frankly, would have done the same if they were in a similar situation. The young couple soon joined a class for young newlyweds. They made lifetime friendships with people that were going through the same joys and trials. The best part was that the change was easy and not awkward for anyone.

Find out from your small group pastor or director what that schedule is for the coming year. If your church does not have such a schedule, you may consider including specific days that are on and off ramps to your group. Once you have the dates, add them to your calendar. If you are depending on a spreadsheet geek from your group to help, this is about when he or she will begin color coding things. Just humor them.

Schedule The Study Content

At this point, your calendar is looking kind of full. This is good. The goal is to plan out every one of the fifty-two group days for the year. Once you have holidays, big days, and church small group schedule days on the calendar, you are ready to start plugging in the content that you will be studying for the year. Remember to go back to what you learned in the discussion with your group. Consider their needs and desires when it comes to studying God's word and choosing curriculum.

For some of you, this section may be a moot point because your church prescribes the study material for you. That's fine. Go with it and plug their plan in on your calendar. You will still have things to put on the calendar of which your group needs to be aware. For the rest of us, this is the time that we start looking at curriculum options and how they fit into your plan. There is no one size fits all from this point so I will describe the process as I go through it with my church's schedule. You can make adjustments accordingly to fit your church's plan.

My church, Park Valley Church of Haymarket, Virginia schedules three thirteen week trimesters for small groups. Using three trimesters as opposed to four quarters allows for ample opportunities in the plan for groups to schedule social and ministry events. It also creates a less rigid schedule when it comes to completing studies on time. Our trimesters begin in February, June, and September. We leave December completely open and use January, May, and August to promote groups.

In thirteen weeks, a group can complete two studies if they so desire. I'm a big fan of the six-week study. We are a culture of short attention spans. We like to get to the point and move on. Beyond six weeks, it is my opinion that people are ready to move on. In a thirteen week trimester, you can easily complete two six weeks or an eight week and a four week. Planning multiple studies within the scheduled time will also allow your group to cover more topics. Leaders will not be burdened by choosing whose needs and desires for group study are going to be met. No need to worry that someone's idea is left out. It also keeps things interesting, always new, and always changing.

If you are following this or a similar schedule, you will most likely have four to six studies to plug in at this point. Once you have covered twelve weeks per trimester, you still have an extra week to plan. The most obvious use for it is to make up a lost week (snow day, holiday, mass alien abduction, whatever). You can also be a little more intentional and schedule a social event or ministry opportunity between the two studies. I recommend this over the make-up day. Your group needs these events to bond and you can schedule another day to make up missed lessons.

Schedule Intentional Days

The final part of the plan for next year is, in my opinion, the most important part. If life change happens in the context of relationships, the remaining days are optimal to facilitate the forming of deeper friendships. Be very intentional in planning opportunities for your group to experience this. In the three trimester schedule, there are a total of three extra months to plan out. At first glance, this seems difficult. When you break it down, it is easier than it looks. The simplest of these months is December. Obviously, Christmas is coming, everyone is busy, and your inclination is to say, "Merry Christmas, see you in January." But Christmas and the New Year is a great time to celebrate what God has done in your group throughout the year. Many people are already in that sentimental, dreaming of a white Christmas kind of mood so why not capitalize on it. I recommend two distinct opportunities—one fellowship, one ministry.

The fellowship is obvious—Christmas party. Have fun. Do the gift exchange and ugly sweaters. Drink eggnog. Break out the Carpenter's Christmas CD. Make it memorable by looking back at what God has done. Give group members time to share. Thank them for remaining faithful and be grateful for their contribution to community.

Also be intentional this time of year when it comes to serving. Between Thanksgiving and Christmas, most churches have opportunities to get involved in some kind of ministry. Sign up as a group to be greeters at the Christmas Eve service. Help collect clothing and blankets for a homeless ministry. Stuff shoe boxes for children in underdeveloped countries. The opportunities are endless. Don't miss out on the chance to serve together as a group.

Once you have the plan for December, go back to the other two months. If that month includes January like it does for my church, you may only have two or three meetings to plan out. A week or so to rest and recuperate from the holidays is a good thing. Put that break on the calendar. Remember, every day has a purpose. Assuming this is a month that is not part of your church's small group schedule, you can purposefully designate the remaining three days as times for social events, ministry, or prayer. Keep them simple. You just finished a busy month and are about to gear up for new studies. No one needs anything complicated.

Finally, you have one more month to plan—May on my books. This is always a great time for us. Groups have been on a role for several weeks. You've gained some momentum so you want to take advantage of that. If that extra month is May or June, this is a great time to add an extra, short study. There are many four week studies available. Publishers seem to be figuring out that our attention spans are only getting shorter and they are providing plenty of small group studies that fit in a single month. If your group loves the service and ministry aspect, take advantage of the nicer weather to get outside and do some outside work. Children's homes, rehab centers, and other residential ministries always need landscaping and painting done.

Plan For Summer

Summer presents its own set of challenges when it comes to small groups. Vacation schedules, camps, and a host of other activities compete for a place on the calendar. Though it seems logical to cancel for the summer, I think this is one of the worst things you can do for your group. You needlessly miss many opportunities to benefit from group life by taking a summer hiatus.

Let's break it down. Taking the summer off generally means that your group will not meet for the months of June, July, and August, or something close to that. That's thirteen weeks. In most places, kids are in school until the second or third week of June. That's two to three weeks you could still meet. July rolls around and vacations start in full force. Fourth of July weekend is a bust. The kids are off to camp. August comes before you know it and everyone starts trickling back into town to get ready for the beginning of school. High school football two-a-days begin early in August and all the other fall sports have brought you back into town for paperwork and practices. School shopping, physicals, arranging carpools, and parent orientation nights have made it necessary for you to be back in town by mid-August. The days may vary from place to place, but the situation is the same for everyone.

In reality, your potential group meetings were only interrupted by four to six weeks. That's less than half the summer leaving six or more weeks that your group can continue to benefit from being together. And as busy as all that sounded, you could probably use the fellowship and prayer to recover!

I'm not suggesting that you pick an intense study and dig in. But it is worth pointing out that there is still time to be together with a group of people that know you well and love you anyway. Movie nights, BBQs, and pool parties are a great way to stay connected with your group through the summer. However, if you are not intentional, it is less likely to happen. And let's face it; we grow closer together in times like this. Potential group members are more comfortable in these situations as well, so invite new people.

Summer months are also a great time to get involved as a group in your community. Nothing says we love you to the people in your community than to see members of your church caring about the same things they care about. School and community improvement opportunities are a great way to make

Jesus and your church known outside the four walls of your church. There are groups from our church that show up on opening day of community baseball and soccer leagues to hand out water and free hot dogs. No intense conversations or invitations are necessary. A church T-shirt and a big smile is the only sermon anyone needs while dragging their kid across the hot parking lot to a mid-morning soccer game.

Take advantage of the summer months to grow closer to your group and become more like Jesus together.

4 THE CLOCK IS TICKING

Why are you standing here, staring into heaven?
Acts 1:9

I love my family. We are not perfect. Like any family, we have our share of problems and challenges. Melinda and I have five children. Beautifully chaotic was the norm in our home. All of our kids are intelligent, creative, active, and full of life. There is a constant buzz of noise and activity—piano, guitar, singing, laughing, and toy guns can be heard at any moment of the day and sometimes well into the night when Melinda tells me to put the toy guns away. Rarely is there a moment of silence in our busy home. I wouldn't change it for the world.

When Melinda and I started our family, we started out knowing that it would not stay the same. Kids will grow into adults. They will bring home young men and women with the intention of adding them to the family. They will move away and begin their own families. In time, the house will be filled with a new chaos. Our kids will bring their kids to our home. Our family will multiply. We knew this from the beginning.

When this process of multiplication begins, it will, no doubt, be accompanied by a fair amount of pain. As I am writing this, I can't help but think that in twenty-nine days, my eighteen-year-old son will ship off to basic training. Soon after that, my twenty-year-old son will return to school about twelve hours away. My twenty-two-year old daughter has plans to be a missionary overseas. I couldn't be more proud of my kids. When it is time for them to leave, I know it is going to hurt.

I have anticipated their growing and inevitable departure from the beginning. On their first day of life, I sat alone in the hospital room, holding each new life while Melinda slept. In this quiet moment, I gave each of my five kids back to God, not that they were ever mine to begin with. God is their Father. I am but a temporary caregiver. Not a day has gone by that we have not prayed for our kids. Melinda and I knew that someday our kids would leave the nest. This is part of life. It is part of raising a family.

Your small group is no different. It is made up of people that will grow and mature. They will come to have influence on other people. At some point, they will leave the nest. This is the nature of people and therefore the nature of groups. Why not capitalize on it. Why not use what comes naturally to expand the influence of your group and its members. If I were describing this as a business model, you might think, double the influence—double the profit. That's exciting! Let's get equally excited about multiplying groups to multiply our influence in God's kingdom.

Before I go on, let me say that I am not without emotion when it comes to multiplying groups. It is hard. It is emotional. It can be like choosing a new family. Recently, Melinda and I saw the need for a group for young, newly married couples in our church. There were several couples that we had gotten to know that were struggling to connect with other people their age. Ours is a large church. There may be many people like you, but it is not always easy to find them. Knowing this, we took it upon ourselves to start this group. We chose a great study on marriage, published the group in our small group database and sent out an email. Our first night we had three couples plus Melinda and me. For the next three or four weeks, we added a couple every week. In short time, we had eight young couples and a few more planning to attend at a later time. We were having a blast. They were young and full of questions. The discussions were lively. We prayed for job changes, pregnancies, and family stuff. Group was supposed to end at 8:30. We usually did not wrap up until 9:30, talking and laughing, crying and praying. They would leave. An hour later I would open the door to let the dog out and the young couples would be standing in our driveway, still talking and laughing.

Melinda and I were reminded of the group of young couples we connected to after we were married and how important that was to us. Many of them are still among our closest friends.

But, twenty is no longer a small group. We were larger than most churches in Southeast Asia. It had been only three months but it was time. We invited two of the couples to dinner. Over dessert, we explained to them that it was necessary to multiply into two groups, each of the two couples taking the lead. They cried. Even the guys cried. Melinda cried. I cried. We had something special, but we knew it was time.

A week or two later, we broke the news to the rest of the group. They cried. There is nothing easy about breaking ties with people you love. I get that. But the results were good. There were now two groups. There was room for growth. Both groups were relocated to places that were more convenient (some members were traveling an hour to meet at our home). The two groups would meet together once a month to hang out. The best result of multiplying, in my opinion, was that members that were less likely to speak in the larger group were now contributing to the conversation. That is a big win in my book.

So when I explain what it means to plan to multiply, I have no direction on how to do this without pain. Nevertheless, multiply you must. It may not be easy but, if done intentionally, it will further the Kingdom and broaden the influence of your group.

Multiplication grows the Church

As a younger pastor, I remember reading articles and books that referred to the new phenomenon of small groups. From where I was perched at the time, only rogue churches sanctioned meetings outside the four walls of the church building—and on weekdays, mind you. Forsaking the Sabbath, they ceased to call them Sunday school classes and began calling them small groups, community groups, and life groups. They were breaking the mold. Defying tradition. They were purpose driven. How dare they!

As God chipped away my ridged, tapered haired, hymn singing, fundamentalist upbringing I began to realize that small groups were not a new thing. In fact, some of the greatest movements of the church throughout history included a small group component. This included the earliest church movement. The very foundation of God's church began with a small group component.

> *"And every day, in the Temple and from house to house, they continued to teach and preach this message: "Jesus is the Messiah." Acts 5:42*

I would someday love to visit the Holy Land but cannot say that I've even been close. I have been in other countries however and can say that most of the world does not enjoy spacious living like we do in the US. Every home that I have visited in other countries could be featured on the show Tiny House Nation. I can only imagine that Jerusalem is no different. Meeting house to house would necessitate a small group of people.

These small groups were not an anomaly. They were foundational to the church and the trend continued. Small groups were a cornerstone of the Reformation. John Calvin and John Wesley both employed the use of small groups to bring the gospel to the people. The Puritans depended on small group meetings to continue worshipping God in opposition to the mandates of the English Church.

Countless homes secretly hosted groups of worshippers under the rule of communism.

I had the brief privilege to work with a Cuban pastor in Miami, Florida. He had only three years prior to our meeting fled Cuba under the threat of persecution. His ministry in Cuba was to serve believers in a network of secret house churches. According to this dear man, the Church in Cuba was alive, healthy and growing.

In modern America, the small group movement is an integral part of some of the fastest growing and largest churches in the county. Andy Stanley, Rick Warren and many others continue to credit the growth and health of their churches to a thriving small group ministry.

The one characteristic that all of these examples throughout history share is that multiplication of groups grows the church. Wesley felt that multiplying groups was the best practice for recruiting new leaders, provided an effective port of entry for new people, and was the best way to involve believers in spreading the gospel. (Comiskey, 2015) And churches that effectively utilize multiplying groups today would wholeheartedly agree. Multiplying groups grows the church.

Make multiplication a part of your group's DNA

Multiplying is something we do. That has to be the attitude of everyone in your group. Your group's mission is the same as the mission of the Church: go and make disciples. I often think of that moment when Jesus ascended into heaven after just having told them to "go". I love the Acts 1 account. As they are staring into the sky watching Jesus ascend, two men in white robes show up.

"Why are you standing here staring into heaven? Jesus has been taken from you into heaven, but someday he will return from heaven in the same way you saw him go!"

Acts 1:11

Before Jesus was completely gone, the disciples were given a reminder that they had a job to do and that the clock was ticking. If the two men had not shown up, the disciples may have started saying things like,

But we need each other
We're like a family
Our kids play so well together

This is a natural response when it comes to multiplying your group. But the reality is that the world needs Jesus more than your group members need each other.

Throughout his ministry, Jesus spoke of his death, burial, and resurrection with the disciples. They didn't know all the details but they knew that it was coming. It was part of their DNA. Jesus will leave. We will spread the gospel.

To make multiplication part of your group's DNA, four things should be happening on a regular basis at your group meetings.
Pray about multiplying

Everything should begin and end with prayer and

your group's plan to multiply shouldn't be any different. Your group prays every week, whether you are praying for each other, the meal, or other requests. Simply add multiplication to your prayer list and be specific.

Plan to invite new people

The simplest way to multiply a group is to create the need for multiplication by inviting new people. An intentional plan for this will make it easy for group members to reach out to new people. Without a plan, there is a natural hesitancy on the part of group members. They are afraid to upset the apple cart by including someone new into your tight-knit group. If you have a plan for inviting new people, all apprehension is removed because new people are expected and welcomed.

There are three places in your overall plan that best accommodate inviting guests to your group: The beginning of a small group semester, between studies, and at an intentionally social event

The beginning of a semester is the best, in my opinion. Most likely your church is already promoting groups to some degree. If you are inviting someone that attends or is new to your church, they are already aware and probably considering the idea of joining a group. Most people just need that personal invite. However, inviting people that don't go to your church or that don't know Jesus, is an awesome opportunity. Remember, your group is the Church. The Great Commission applies to groups.

Prior to the beginning of a new semester, plan a day that is primarily social in nature. Include a lot of food, fun, and fellowship. If you have access to a promotional video for the upcoming study, plan to show it. Intentionally make this an opportunity for guests to see that group is family. Groups do life together and care about each other. They rely on the Bible to help with everyday problems. If guests see that the group members depend on this time every week, they will be more inclined to share in that special, intimate time with you.

Mid-semester, you may be moving to a new study as your current study comes to an end. Plan to incorporate a meeting like the one described in the previous paragraphs. If your group is flexible as to the study you choose, choose a study that has a broader appeal—something that your guests would want to be a part of. Everyday life issues are a great choice. Most people are looking for help with parenting, marriage, dating, and money. Topics such as these are more attractive than digging into a book of the Bible or a study of doctrine. Certainly, groups should be digging into the scripture but felt need topics are often a better choice to connect new people with your group. As they acclimate to group life, in time they will appreciate digging deeper into God's word.

At this point, inviting people to an intentionally social event may seem redundant. The events we've already discussed are social in nature. The difference between this and what we've already talked about is that they take place on holidays or in the summer and may not precede a new study. These are great opportunities to invite people that are new believers or new to your church. Some people, new believers especially, are a little creeped out by the idea of joining a small group. Inviting them to join you for a Labor Day cookout, however, is perceived as a friendly gesture as opposed to a cult-ish ploy to join a community of followers.

Okay, that was a little over the top. Nevertheless, people, in general, are looking for friends so a casual invite to a cookout, pool party, movie night or whatever is a great way to connect new people to your group. Follow the evening up with an informal, "Hey, we do this every week," kind of invitation and you will be surprised at the response you will get.

Be sure to include your group in planning these guest-appropriate meetings. Let them be in on inviting and preparing for guests. Ask for their input on making it a great evening and make sure they understand the purpose. If multiplication is part of your DNA they will know that they are part of a bigger plan—God's plan.

Pick New Leaders

Nobody likes to volunteer. When someone asks for volunteers it usually means that no one else is willing to do it. If you ask your group members, "who wants to lead a group," take a moment to sit back and enjoy the chorus of crickets because that is probably all you will hear. There are better ways to pick new leaders.

In political science, there is a term referred to as the leadership vacuum. Putting it simply, a leadership vacuum is a lack of leadership. In a leadership vacuum, two things can happen—chaos or new leadership naturally steps up. As a group leader, you can discover new leaders by intentionally creating a leadership vacuum. I'm not implying that you abandon your group all-together. Instead, intentionally creating the need for new leadership causes potential leaders to emerge. As they emerge you can see who is capable of leading a group. One of the best ways to plan a vacuum is to invite someone to lead when you are not available. At some time during the year, you will not be available on group night. Most leaders opt for canceling group and group members are all too eager to agree. Instead, invite someone to lead in your absence. Take advantage of a single leadership vacuum to develop new leaders.

When I recently started a group of married couples with kids, I let them know that we would take prayer requests at every meeting. I intentionally did not write them down—a leadership vacuum. At the second meeting, someone said, "Can I write these down and email them to everyone?" Boom! Long story short, she is now leading a small group for homeschool moms.

In other words, if you take it upon yourself to do everything for your group, then no one else will do anything. I once spoke to a leader of a group that did exactly that for a long time. She was the teacher, the organizer, the prayer leader, the caregiver, etc. Her group members were all mature Christians. Some were on staff at the church. She begged and pleaded for people to take on tasks. They did not. This continued for nearly two years. She asked me how she should handle it. Though I would not give this advice to everyone, I told her to leave the group and start a new one. She did. The group was in limbo for a time, but before too long they reorganized. They were now two groups—three including the one the former leader started. Everyone took on new responsibilities. Again, this was a unique group of people that knew the value of group life, so it was safe to take such drastic measures. But in the end, a vacuum of leadership caused new leaders to rise to the top and more groups were launched.

Another way to develop new leaders is to simply hand pick them. As you get to know the people in your group, you will notice those that are more mature believers and capable leaders. Because multiplication is part of your DNA, this person will not be surprised when you ask them. They may even be waiting for that invitation. Your church may have standards that must be met before someone can lead. By all means, stick to those standards. Your church leadership has created them for a reason. However, we are, in the broadest sense, called to do two things—love God and love people. If someone genuinely has those two characteristics then they possess this potential leadership ability. Look for those qualities first.

Plan to keep the small in small group

It is exciting to see your group grow. Growth is an indicator of life and health. It means God is blessing and people are using their gifts to reach out to others. But there is a difference between healthy growth and overcrowding.

I like to garden. I'm no good at it but I still enjoy it. I like that I can drop a few seeds on the ground, care for them, and a few months later I can put dinner on the table. That's a good feeling. I also learn things the hard way. I don't follow directions well and often think I know more than the guy on the YouTube gardening video that I watched. Last summer, I planted a variety of squash-zucchini, yellow squash, and acorn squash to name a few. The guy on the video said that I should make a mound of dirt and plant about 6-8 seeds on each mound. Once they sprout, remove half of them and leave the half that looks the healthiest. In my mind, if six to eight is good, then ten to twelve must be awesome! If they all look healthy, don't remove any. What I ended up with was a tangled mess of vines that choked each other out and crowded out the rest of the garden. The lettuce and cabbage didn't stand a chance against the serpent-like stranglehold of the killer squash. In other words, my garden became so overcrowded that it became unhealthy. Other vegetables were overshadowed and incapable of growth. Having fewer squash creates a healthier environment that encourages growth.

Like my pitiful garden, when your group becomes too big it ceases to be healthy. I'm convinced that all groups are small groups no matter how large or small they are. A group of thirty is really a small group of ten with twenty spectators. About ten people do all the talking. Generally, they are the ones that participate, pray, read scripture, and answer questions while everyone else quietly watches. People that need to speak do not have the opportunity. They cannot share what God is doing, where they are struggling, or how they can help someone else. They miss out on the blessing of intimate relationships and close fellowship. A group that surpasses ten people needs to multiply to give those people an opportunity to be blessed and to be a blessing.

The clock is ticking

The two men in white made it clear to the disciples that time is ticking away and there is a lot to do. We don't have the luxury of waiting until it is comfortable to multiply. Set multiplication goals within your group. Andy Stanley made a plea to his church that all groups plan to multiply within twelve to eighteen months of their launch date. He did the math right there on stage. (Stanley, 2004) The numbers were ridiculous, far surpassing the numbers in his church at the time. If they even got to 50% of the numbers he was rattling off, they would still have reached thousands of people with the gospel.

A group that is not intentionally planning to multiply is a group that is inadvertently planning to become unhealthy, stagnant, and ineffective. Communicate the need for a healthy environment to your group. Let them know that there is a limit to the number of people in a healthy group. As they are growing and inviting new people to attend, the goal is to create an atmosphere that encourages spiritual growth. Multiplying is key to creating this environment.

5 WRONG BAIT, RIGHT POND

People join a small group for content, but they stay for the relationships. – Rick Warren

Life was great when I was a kid. The world still seemed like a friendly place. Every summer day was an adventure for my friends and me and the entire neighborhood was our playground. Neighbors watched out for each other. There was no need for gates or guards or neighborhood watch.

The typical summer day meant rolling out of bed early, grabbing a pop tart, fishing pole and tackle box, a handful of night crawlers and running to the pond. On the way, my brother Tom and I knocked on the doors of friends' homes inviting them to join us on the adventure. The rest of the day we spent fishing. And we were great at it. Most days we would each bring home five or six bluegill, perch, and the occasional catfish. When the supply at the pond no longer met our demand we moved on to the creek up the road. When the creek was no longer productive we sneaked into the back side of Taylor's pond. Old man Taylor (we called him that but he was probably in his forties) did not want us fishing from his pond. We did it anyway. The catch from this covert operation was the most productive of all our fishing holes. We were expert anglers. The fish didn't stand a chance.

Life goes on. I grew up, got married, left the freshwater streams and ponds of Virginia and moved to South Florida. Our home was a mile from the beach. We started a family. When my sons were old enough, I knew it was time to pass on my vast knowledge and expertise of fishing to them. We grabbed pop tarts, fishing poles, and tackle boxes and off we went. I had no experience in ocean fishing so we went to more familiar territory—the Loxahatchee River. On the way, we stopped to buy nightcrawlers. I demonstrated my mad skills of baiting a hook to the boys. Mouths gagging and eyes watering, they eventually baited their own hooks. We tossed our lines into the water and waited...and waited. Certainly, something would take our bait. Not so. I pulled my line in to inspect the bait. Perhaps it fell off mid-cast. Wrong. It was still there. What used to be a meaty buffet of plump nightcrawler was now a sagging mass of limp, shriveled flesh that no fish would covet. I re-baited and cast again. Still nothing. Same result. Eventually, my boys said, "I'm bored, let's go to the beach!" I was devastated.

The lesson I learned that day was that the bait that works well in the freshwater streams in Virginia does not work in the brackish waters of South Florida. You must have the right bait in the right place to attract a fish. The curriculum or Bible studies you choose for your group are very much like bait. They can attract people to your group or drive them away. They can keep group members engaged or give them a reason to leave. Fishing requires an understanding of the environment and the fish. The same is true in understanding your group.

If you are starting a new group, finding the right study can be particularly difficult. If you do not know the people you will not be able to anticipate what their specific needs and desires are. However, this does not have to handicap you as a group leader. You can still zero in on good choices by answering the following questions.

What does your community look like?

Having spent over twenty years in South Florida and recently returning to Northern Virginia, the similarities and differences in the two communities were immediately obvious. South Florida is a laid back, working for the weekend kind of atmosphere. Northern Virginia is high pressure, working to get that next promotion kind of environment. South Floridians spend ten to fifteen hours a week on the beach or on a boat. Northern Virginians spend fifteen to twenty hours a week commuting to and from work. Neither could be described as Bible-belt communities. Both are diversely ethnic and under-churched. That bit of information alone narrows down the choice of study material tremendously.

Because of the hectic lifestyle, most people in Northern Virginia will not commit to a months-long study that requires daily homework. Excruciating two-hour commutes make it complicated for many to find even an hour in the evening to attend a group. The stress of careers puts an enormous strain on marriages and family life. In general, short, easily accessible studies that offer uncomplicated access to Biblical solutions to everyday problems are the way to encourage people to connect with groups in this high-pressure region of the country. Because of time constraints, people are also looking for recreational outlets. Groups that focus primarily on sports and recreation are one of the best ways to connect people to group life.

South Florida stands in tremendous contrast. The average commute is less than thirty minutes. Traffic is relatively light compared to Northern Virginia. The beach culture provides hours of recreation year round. Marriages seem healthier. People are less likely to have their purpose wrapped up in a career and therefore seek more purpose from life. Though short, easily accessible studies are still appreciated, South Floridians are more likely to engage in long-term commitments to a group or study. They are also more likely to engage in a 'homework' style commitment.

Now that you are well-prepared to lead a group in Northern Virginia or South Florida, let's take a look at your community. Draw a five-mile circle around your church. Within that circle, what is the median age? What is family life like? Would you describe it as churched or unchurched? Is there a university within walking distance? Are there a lot of kids or teens? Is it rural, suburban or urban? The list of questions is endless. If your church leaders have done their homework, they will have the answers to these questions.

Suddenly, this all becomes very obvious. But a failure to consider the question of community will lead to mistakes. A well-intentioned person may launch a new group on raising toddlers in a church that is right in the middle of a retirement community. Another may try to establish a long-term, heavy commitment Bible study among young adults in a college town without considering their schedules and the fact that most of them will be gone in a matter of months.

What does your church look like?

Like the community question, the same information regarding your church is equally as important. If multiplication is truly part of your group's DNA, members of your church and group will be inviting their friends from the community. The same questions as to demographics apply. An even more important question regarding your church is, "where are they spiritually?" If you are in a church full of churched people, a study that goes a little deeper than most may be more appropriate as well as topics such as apologetics, evangelism, and exegetical studies. If you are in a church that has attracted new believers, studies that introduce them to the person of Jesus, the purpose and mission of his church, and assimilation to church life are great places to begin. Millennials are more interested in being the church than they are going to church. Studies that emphasize action and engage them in ministry are a win. Knowing the spiritual temperature of your church is key in choosing study material.

What does your group look like?

If your group is already established, you can probably answer this question like a pro. You probably see the answer in the mirror every morning because groups often represent the same demographic and temperament as their leader. The important consideration concerning your group is to not assume you know what they need. Meeting the needs of the group should be a frequent topic of discussion among your group members. Pay attention to prayer requests. If everyone is praying for financial needs, a study on Biblical finances is an obvious choice.

Be sensitive to their obvious needs. Women's groups are often characterized by homework and daily readings. Preschool moms have little time for this and don't need the pressure. They are at group so that they can have an adult conversation and spend an hour without being covered in spit-up. Hurting people need TLC and answers from God's word over a long period of time. They need the patience of a group that will be there for them no matter what.

My title at the church is Next Step Pastor. We define discipleship as encouraging someone to take their next step in following Jesus. Your group members' "next step" is also worthy of discussion and consideration when choosing material. If your group is full of new believers, studies that discuss baptism, church membership, and other basics of the faith may be the best choice. If you are a group primarily of empty nesters, studies on leaving a legacy, leadership development, and rekindling romance can reenergize a group of people that suddenly have time on their hands and a little peace and quiet around the house. The point is that everyone has a next step to take.

You may also discuss with your group what they perceive as a spiritual deficiency. Where do they feel most inadequate in their relationship with Jesus and their responsibility to share his love? Evangelism is often an area in which believers feel ill-equipped. There are numerous studies on how to share your faith. As the leader, you don't have to be an expert. Just learn along with them. Discussion and prayer will reveal their next steps and help you choose material that will benefit the members of your group.

Once you know the direction your group needs to move or topics they want to cover, then you have the daunting task of choosing the actual study material. I say that it is daunting because there are thousands and thousands to choose from. My church subscribes to an online streaming service that boasts a library of over 10,000 studies. The choices are endless and the prospect of narrowing them down seems nearly impossible. Fortunately, the publishing companies, distributors, and streaming websites want to help you do this. Their websites allow you to search for a particular topic and list them by popularity or highest sales. Popularity and higher sales are often an indication that there is something special about that product.

Word of mouth is another great method of deciding on a particular study. Odds are, someone else in your church has done a study on your chosen topic and can make recommendations. Be sure to ask the right group leader. The group of preschool moms may not get the best curriculum recommendations from the fifty-something divorced men's group. Ask someone who is at the same stage of life or close to it. I also encourage our group leaders to post the names of their favorite studies on our Facebook page and to share the names of studies in small group leader meetings.

Finally, another way to discover the direction for your group is to use a simple survey that asks some direct questions. You can develop your own or use the suggested questions below.

- *What do you think is your next step in following Jesus?*
- *In what area of your life do you feel you need the most help?*
- *What command of scripture do you feel least equipped to obey?*
- *What book or passage of the Bible intrigues you the most?*
- *What topics would you like to discuss at group?*

The last question is so obvious I hesitate to include it. I do not recommend asking this out loud (see chapter one).

Ask these questions of your group about two months prior to developing your group calendar for the year. It will make the planning process much simpler.

A yearlong plan for curriculum

Because we are planning a year's worth of study ahead of time, the conclusions you reach using the questions and concepts we discussed in the first part of this chapter should have multiple implications. The goal is to discover several needs and next steps within your group and to coordinate studies that address those issues. This is best discovered over a reasonable amount of time and many different conversations with your group. Attempting to learn all of this about the group members in a single sitting will be awkward and probably not give you an accurate depiction of what they need. Make this an ongoing discussion and keep notes about their responses. When choosing a year's worth of studies, refer back to the notes you kept to help you plan. You may not be able to use all of the ideas and suggestions, but you will have more than enough to plan out a full year of group meetings.

Right now is the best time to begin this process. Grab a piece of paper and a calendar and start creating your plan. Keep it simple, but include each day that you will meet over the next year. Start by planning just the next three months. You will learn much about planning the rest of the year by creating a short-term, three-month plan.

6 INTENTIONALLY SOCIAL

Fun over time creates connections that make friendships go deeper. Reggie Joiner

Planning to be social sounds a lot like planning to sweat on a hot day—it just kind of happens. For that reason, it almost seems like a topic that needs little attention. But the point of creating the plan is to be intentional with every group meeting, including those that are purely social in nature. Gatherings that are intentionally social present opportunities to develop deeper relationships more than the usual Bible study meetings. Some of the most significant times in Jesus' ministry happened around social gatherings. His first miracle was performed at a wedding reception. The transfiguration took place during the Feast of Shelters. Some of his most intimate moments with the disciples occurred during the Passover celebration. And he challenged Peter, the first leader of the church, over a campfire breakfast of freshly caught fish. Because Jesus is the omniscient God on earth, it is safe to assume that none of this happened by chance and that there was a purpose in pouring into his followers at gatherings characterized by social interaction. It is also safe to assume that intentionally planning social gatherings will benefit the groups that we lead.

As we pointed out in previous chapters, there are a number of opportunities to plan social events and we have discussed some of the ways we can make them more intentional such as inviting new group members. The following discussion will outline a number of reasons why we should be intentionally social. But first, let's consider the obvious elements that a social event might include.

Obvious Element #1: Fellowship

Fellowship has become the Jesus-speak term for social gatherings in general and ninety seconds of handshaking just before the offering is collected on Sunday mornings. Churches all over the planet have gatherings called, "fellowships", for the purpose of social interaction. I went to a million of these in the last half-century and all have their own twist—ice cream fellowship, singles fellowship, wild game fellowship—and the list goes on. By labeling everything a fellowship, we have taken a Biblical term and assigned a non-Biblical description to it. Fellowship more commonly describes an event rather than accurately describing genuine community.

The Biblical term *koinonia* has no literal English translation but is commonly translated as fellowship or communion. *Koinonia* is used to describe the community of fellow believers in Acts 2:42, the generous contribution of the Macedonian church to believers in Jerusalem in Romans 15:24, and the "communion" with Christ that is represented in the elements of the Lord's Supper in 1 Corinthians 10:16. We use the term when describing being unequally yoked in marriage when we say, "what communion hath light with darkness," in 2 Corinthians 6:14. And according to 1 John 1:7, when we "walk in the light as he is in the light," we experience *koinonia* because of Jesus shed blood. The overarching common thread in all of this is the idea of oneness with and in Jesus.

Several years ago I was taking some classes toward a graduate degree at Westminster Choir College in Princeton, New Jersey. I had the option of staying in a local hotel or, if I wanted to save a little money, I could stay in the on-campus dormitory. I was in my thirties, married with kids, and way beyond the age of dorm life. But I am hopelessly tight-fisted when it comes to personal comfort so I chose dorm life. What was I thinking? It was summer so the dorm was not full, but the residents were mostly college-aged kids that regarded me as a decrepit old man. The party was usually just getting started right around my bedtime.

There was, however, a bright spot to this very bad decision to stay in the dorm. When I applied, they noticed that I was from a Christian school, so they tried to match me up with a roommate with similar interests. My roommate for the week was a Korean pastor. When I arrived, I walked into the room to find him on his knees, Bible open and praying passionately. I apologized for interrupting and proceeded to introduce myself. His response was simply, "I don't speak English." I replied loudly and slowly because Americans think that if we speak loudly and slowly the entire world understands us.

"I don't speak Korean." One would assume that this would make for an awkward week of silence and polite nods but quite the opposite happened. Every night as we were turning in, we both opened our Bibles and read silently. Then, just before we turned the lights out, we would pray together-he in Korean and I in English. Each time of prayer was more beautiful and intimate than the night before. I remember being moved to tears by the passion in his voice as he prayed. After a week, it was time for him to leave. I still had a week to go, so we said our farewells and embraced. He looked at me, and in broken English said, "God bless you, brother."

Two men who come from different parts of the world and speak different languages experienced *koinonia*. Not because of long, meaningful conversations or the next scheduled fellowship event, rather, we experienced it because Jesus shed his blood for both of us. We experienced oneness, not because of what we said, but because of what Jesus did. This is the true essence of fellowship.

This kind of fellowship typically happens at two particular times in a small group—prayer time and social time. When praying together, we open up about personal and intimate parts of our lives. We become vulnerable as we share our struggles with the group. When spending time socially, we continue that discussion. We ask the questions that show the ongoing concern for group members.

How are the kids?
How's the job hunt going?
How was the doctor visit?

Because of our oneness through Jesus, we begin to live out the gospel within our group.

Bare one another's burdens
Care for one another
Pray for one another
Encourage one another

And the list goes on. In other words, we do life together. This is authentic fellowship.

Obvious Element #2: Food

I grew up in the Baptist church. Fried chicken and Watergate salad were as sacred as the bread and wine. No one ever said, "Should we serve food?" when planning a church event. It was expected. I think most churches experience this to some degree. Surprisingly, new group leaders often ask, "Should I serve food at group?" My response is almost always yes. The small group I currently attend has dinner together every time we meet. We choose a theme—taco night, breakfast food, or whatever. We love it. We have kids at group so it gives us a chance to interact with them before they go to the basement. One of the girls in our group took on the responsibility of organizing and communicating with the other families about the meal plan. It works for us. I've been in groups that just serve coffee and tea and maybe a light refreshment. In others, we try to wow each other with decadent desserts. You can do whatever works for your group.

There is one big advantage to serving food at group—people are more comfortable when their hands are not dangling awkwardly at their sides during a conversation. This is particularly beneficial when introducing new people to the group. Our church serves coffee and donuts to 2500 people every weekend because of this. This may seem like a small thing, but getting people comfortable in friendly conversation is the first step towards being comfortable in intimate conversations. The business world knows this. Business deals take place at a restaurant as often as they do the boardroom. Food makes people more comfortable. It's that simple. And if the conversation isn't going well, you can always talk about the food.

Obvious Element #3: Planned Fun

I'm the guy that cringes every time someone mentions board games. I hate to lose. I hate waiting my turn. I hate putting down a good chicken wing to roll the dice. However, I will be the first to admit that when I do play board games with friends and family, I have a blast. There is a reason for this.

First, during a board game, conversation is no longer awkward. You have something to talk about—the game. It is easy to loosen up and relax when conversation flows more naturally. Secondly, at some point, everyone is laughing. Nothing breaks down social barriers more than laughter. Finally, if even for a brief moment, everyone is the center of attention when it is their turn. This smacks of self-centeredness, but the reality is we all crave attention. During the board game, we get attention without the awkwardness of being under a microscope. All this and dozens of other reasons can be summed up in one simple statement: its fun.

In his book, "Playing for Keeps", an awesome book about family ministry that has tremendous application to small groups, Reggie Joiner describes the importance of fun.   Using what looks like a mathematical formula, Reggie explains that, "fun over time creates connections that make friendships go deeper." (Joiner, 178) When your group is having fun together, you get to see the less serious side of people.   The normal small group time does not necessarily afford the opportunity to see one's sense of humor, competitive nature, or creativity.   You as the leader must create the opportunity to become more familiar with group members and to create memories.   Think for a moment about the most memorable times from your past.   It's a safe guess that none of those fond memories involve a Sunday school lesson or an algebraic equation.   They probably involve an event characterized by tragedy or fun as opposed to learning.   If fun is deliberate in your group, there is a greater likelihood of strengthening and deepening relationships that could be instrumental in transforming someone's life.

Fun also gives group members something to look forward to. It could be said that all work and no play makes group a dull hour.

Intentionally Social

At the beginning of this chapter, I implied that being social comes naturally, like sweating on a hot day. Being social generally comes naturally to people because we were created that way.   It is my experience, however, that it does not necessarily come naturally to group life and must be cultivated. People at group events will require little encouragement to be social—to carry on conversations, etc. This happens naturally. But the idea of being intentionally social as a group does not come naturally. In fact, given the choice to plan a social event or not meet, most groups will opt to not meet. It's simply more convenient. We tell ourselves, "everyone could use the break." Break from what? If your group needs a break, maybe it's time to improve what your group is doing. I've never heard a committed football fan say, "Man, I just need a break from Monday Night Football." On the other hand, I have seen grown men driven to tears because their team did not make the playoffs, thus cutting short his reason for living by about a month.

I am not implying that our groups should meet fifty-two weeks a year and that we are weak and ineffective if we choose not to meet. Yes, there are times that our families should be together instead of at group and when it has been a busy week and we could just use a quiet evening at home. There are plenty of those times whether we take them together or as individuals. The point of being intentionally social is to create opportunities that deepen and strengthen our group—to make our groups healthy.

Imagine if the church you attended met weekly, sang, preached, collected the offering, and went home. Repeat. Week after week. Nothing else. No matter how good the preaching and music is, after a while, you and every other warm body at the church will start craving more. You will cease to find satisfaction in the weekly experience and lack of interaction with others. In time, you will need a break. Now, imagine how it is in reality. Add to the weekly schedule of singing and preaching, an ongoing effort to reach the community. On top of that, include regularly scheduled potlucks, picnics, and prayer breakfasts. Suddenly, the weekly schedule feels less sterile. There is more opportunity to interact with others. Though the additions to the schedule serve other purposes, they are all social in nature. And they are intentional. They are on the calendar for a reason.

Why should our groups be any different? Why should they be all business and no play? There are tremendous advantages to being intentionally social in our groups.

Create Anticipation

Being intentionally social gives group members something to look forward to. Several years ago, when our kids were younger, my wife and I bit the bullet and bought annual family passes to Disney as Christmas presents to our kids. They also got a puppy and a drum set. What was I thinking? We only lived two hours from Orlando so we could drive up for the day and then turn around and come home. Because we were a homeschool family, we could go anytime we wanted. We ended up going two or three times a month—sometimes more. Every birthday was celebrated at one of the parks. Melinda and I even pawned the kids off on friends and went by ourselves. It was a pretty cool year. By the end of the year, I remember one of our kids asking, "Do we have to go to Disney?"

One thing Melinda and I learned quickly is that if you tell the kids too far in advance that you are going to

Disney, they will bug you about it continuously until you get in the car to leave. We started telling them as we tucked them in at night, "Oh, by the way, we are going to Disney tomorrow!" Telling them in advance created an exciting sense of anticipation that they could not control. That's just the way people are. This is an attribute that is easy to take advantage of in small groups. Too often the potential social events are discussed in reaction to the failure of the normal group meeting.

> *The Jones and the Maxwells are not coming this weekend.*
> *Too bad. No point in doing the next chapter.*
> *What if we just cook out?*
> *I don't know. It's kind of a busy weekend.*
> *You're right. We need a break anyway.*

A break from the monotony is what you need! Planning a purely social event in advance will be met with much more enthusiasm than the discussion above could ever generate. Imagine this discussion:

> *Our small group calendar says that we are cooking out at our house in three weeks.*
> *I'm making my famous BBQ sauce!*
> *I spoke to the Maxwell's. They are going to visit the group and might join us for the next study.*
> *Who's bringing the Lawn Darts?*

This is obviously more positive than the previous discussion. And you can't go wrong with Lawn Darts! Even though it is just a cookout, there is a sense of anticipation because it is out of the ordinary. Creating a sense of anticipation requires planning ahead.

Opportunity for Growth

Our church is very casual in nature. Like many modern churches, we have opted for jeans and T-shirts over coats and ties. To explain this part of our culture, our pastor frequently asks, "are you more comfortable at a formal dinner or a picnic?" This question could be asked concerning guests attending your group for the first time. Consider where they would be the most comfortable. In small group life, our formal dinner is the normal time of sharing and discovering God's word together. Rather than inviting them to something that could potentially make them uncomfortable, invite them to something less intimidating like a group movie night or Labor Day cookout. Consider the difference between the two events. At your weekly Bible study, they enter your house and are greeted by the host and introduced to other group members. Perhaps they are given a snack and something to drink. Sounds good so far, but my guess is they are thinking, "I feel terrible. We should have brought something." They continue to make small talk until it is time to go to the living room for the Bible study and discussion time. They find their place, the group prays and the awkwardness begins.

Should I say something?
What if they ask me a question?
Why didn't anyone ask me a question?

And the list of awkward feelings continues.

Not only is this awkward for your guest, but it can also be awkward for the rest of the group. They may be less likely to share things they would have under normal circumstances. Their conversation is a little less transparent.

To invite them first to a casual, socially oriented event presents far less pressure on everyone. Except for the group leader, no one is ever the sole focus of attention. No one has to speak to the group. It is a great chance to get to know the potential members.

Making Memories

As our kids get older they are all going their own separate ways. Melinda and I treasure every moment we have when all the kids are together. It does not matter what we plan to do as a family, the brief times that we spend together nearly always end in all of us sitting around the dining room table talking about our favorite memories. Oddly enough, the trips to Disney never come up. We talk about times that may have seemed insignificant at the time. Mostly, we talk about times that made us laugh. Though there were many times that we cried together, fought with each other, and shared struggle and pain, our greatest and fondest memories involve laughter.

As the leader of your group, it is important to create the opportunity for those times. Yes, these moments will happen naturally to some extent. But planning time for your group to experience fun together creates the memories that connect you to the group members over time. Those are the moments that strengthen relationships and ultimately help to build trust. Including a social element, or fun, to your group plan is always a win.

7 COMMUNICATE WELL AND OFTEN

Communication leads to community, that is, to understanding, intimacy and mutual valuing.
-Rollo May

Earlier in this book, I mentioned that my son would soon be leaving for basic training. That day has come and gone and is but a simple memory compared to what I have experienced since. Jacob finished basic training after nine or ten weeks and eventually went on to jump school and is now part of the 82nd Airborne. My chest swells a little every time I say that. As I am writing this paragraph, I am sitting in a rented room at Fort Bragg, North Carolina, just a stone's throw from Pope Air Field. I am up late waiting to hear the roar of multiple jets flying overhead. On one of those jets will sit my son Jacob. His first destination is Kuwait and then Mosul, Iraq. My chest still swells, but now it is because my heart is so full of emotions. Jacob has been trained to fight, and fight he most likely will. We said our tearful goodbyes to Jake tonight and watched him file on to a bus with a few dozen other soldiers. There were eight to ten other white buses filling up as well. We stood and watched from the sidewalk. We could see Jake make his way to the back of the bus and find his seat. His face was still red from the tears he shed as he said goodbye to his family and his precious girlfriend. There were hundreds of weepy families around us. He sat down and not a moment later my phone dinged. It was a group text from Jake. "I love you guys!" We all began texting back and forth.

We love you, too.
Praying for you.
We'll miss you

In that lightened moment, I realized that I am truly thankful to God for technology. Simple apps on my phone enable me to stay in touch with my son when he is living in a make-shift bunker on the other side of the planet. If I can stay connected to my son from such great a distance, then we are without excuse when it comes to connecting with our group during the week. I am the "chief of sinners" when it comes to this, in spite of the fact that staying in touch is as simple as sending a group text or email. I have recently become very grateful for the technology that enables us to remain connected.

For many like myself, staying connected requires an intentional effort. I am not a small talk kind of guy. I rarely call someone just to chat. I'm just not wired that way. Those who are inclined instinctively to stay connected to group members seem to be rare. I think most people need to be deliberate in their efforts to stay connected. The plan can be very simple and still be effective.

Plan a Time

Choosing a regular day and time to reach out to your group members is helpful to you as the leader and to your group members. I make a point to reach out to my small group leaders at church every Tuesday afternoon. Most often I send an email thanking them for investing in the lives of others and to communicate any opportunities on the horizon. I will also take the time to post something on our group leader Facebook page. Keeping this routine encourages me to be consistent in my efforts to connect with them. In turn, my group leaders have also come to expect something from me on Tuesdays. Choose a regular day and time to reach out to your group and you will find that it becomes much easier to stay connected outside of scheduled group times.

Plan a Medium

Thirty years ago there were only a couple of options when it came to communication. In the last two decades, electronic media has not only replaced the telephone and snail mail, it has made them nearly obsolete. I used to look forward to going to the mailbox. A card or letter was always a treat. Now it's just bills and junk mail. I will go days without checking the mail. Today, the number of options for simple communication is staggering and they are different with every demographic. It appears that my generation tapped into email and Facebook, two options that apparently make me look like an old man to my kids. Their primary means of communication is texting and Snap Chat. At least it is today. Whatever medium you choose is fine as long as it is effective. If you are using a medium that no one else uses, it is pointless and your efforts to convert them to your favorite app will probably prove to be ineffective. Choose a medium to which they are most accustomed and stick with it. Also, do not over-communicate by using multiple media. In the end, your group members may become irritated and pay less attention to what is being said. A single medium at an appointed day and time will speak louder than a barrage of pings from multiple applications.

Plan a Purpose

Time is precious and no one appreciates it when someone else wastes it. Receiving too many emails is frustrating. Pointless emails are just as annoying. According to the website for DMR Digital Statistics and Graphics, the average office employee receives 121 emails per day. (Robbins, 2018) Add to that texts, Facebook and Instagram hits, and phone calls. Your efforts to communicate are important so you want them to get through. If the majority of your emails or texts are without purpose, the ones that have a purpose will be dismissed before they are read.

Unnecessarily long communication can also be frustrating. We are a culture of short attention spans. If someone opens an email message and finds a small novel, it will end up in the recycle bin in quick order. Keep group communication purposeful, short, and to the point. If there are men in your group, bullet points are even better. Just sayin'.

Having a plan to stay connected begins with regular,

purposeful communication but it does not end there. Some people in your group may need extra attention during challenging and painful times. Meeting a group member for coffee, phone calls, etc. is necessary from time to time. However, your group members may begin doing this on their own with each other. This is an indication of a healthy group that does life together.

Intentional Communication Shows You Care

I have a thirty-year-old shoe box upstairs full of letters from Melinda. We were college sweethearts. The year before we were married Melinda lived in Orlando and I lived two and half hours away in Jupiter. There was still such a thing as long distance calls. They could be expensive so we were not able to talk daily. We depended on writing letters and the U.S. Postal Service to communicate. I knew that Melinda cared about me because she communicated it to me in those letters. We were 150 miles apart and spoke about once a week, but that did not stop us. We still communicated and we knew that we cared about each other.

Communicating in your small group will demonstrate to them that you care about them. A weekly email or occasional phone call will speak volumes to your group members about your commitment to them individually as opposed to your commitment to the group.

Intentional Communication Deepens Relationships

Not only did I know how that Melinda cared, but her letters made it clear how much she cared for me. I fell more and more in love with her with every perfume-laced letter. Communication has a way of building trust and intimacy. When couples begin to drift apart, it usually begins with a lack of communication.

The same drift may happen in your group if there is little communication outside of group. Let's face it. Your group members are not coming because you are a great speaker or learned scholar. They can hear the best of preaching and teaching twenty-four/seven thanks to the internet. They are coming because they have the need for deep relationships. You may be a great teacher, but that will only go so far. Our group members crave intimacy. Being intentional with communication encourages that kind of intimacy among small group members.

Intentional Communication Creates Trust

Prayer requests are a no-brainer in small groups. We all do it. We all expect it. However, once group is over, it's often not much more than a list that may be easily forgotten. One of the most effective things you can do as a group leader is to call and pray with your group members outside of group time.

In our church in Florida, our deacons were all assigned a group of people to shepherd. Doug was my deacon and a good friend. Our kids grew up together, our wives homeschooled together, and we served together in children's ministry. But I could say that about a dozen people in that church. What set Doug apart from others was the fact that Doug checked up on me on a regular basis to pray for me. That meant the world to me. Knowing that Doug prayed for me made it easy to trust him. I could tell Doug about struggles I was having. I confided in Doug concerning some difficult things that were happening in ministry. A simple act of communication that included, "how can I pray for you," created a significant trust between us.

Everyone in your group is going through something. They may talk about it in group or they may not. But you can guarantee that everyone has a situation that needs prayer. As leaders, we must be intentional about connecting with our group members through prayer. Job losses, illnesses, issues with our kids and a million other hurts are why prayer needs to be an intentional part of communication with your group.

8 REGULAR CHECK-UPS

*We never grow closer to God when we just live life.
It takes deliberate pursuit and attentiveness.*
Francis Chan

I recently turned fifty. Men older than I congratulated me and welcomed me to, "the club". I assumed that by being part of this club that I would experience a new level of manliness and comradery that a man in his forties was not ready for—a cigar smoking clutch of surly kinsman that would hereafter define real manhood. What I found was a bunch of guys talking about their latest, "procedure" and making desperate attempts to undo the damage they had done to their bodies over the last twenty years. They join gyms and buy expensive exercise equipment. They go to doctors that specialize in the unthinkable. It was a frightening, almost horrifying transition for me, the carefree man-boy that eats red meat and bacon like it's my last meal on death row. Suddenly being intentionally healthy was a priority. Ok, not so much for me, but for most of the 50+ guys I hang out with.

Health is important to your group too. Not the put on yoga pants and eat your veggies kind of health, but spiritual health. Like so many things, I have learned this lesson the hard way.

Several years ago, our church adopted a paradigm for small groups that transformed the way we did groups. It focused on aggressively getting people to connect with community on any level. We considered nearly anything to be a group as long as people were signing up for it. In no time, we doubled the number of groups and then doubled them again. It was awesome. We had nearly 85% of our regular attendees in some kind of group. The national average is less than 40%. (Earls, 2014)

Then, the bottom fell out. In six months we lost half of the new groups. Three months later we lost half of what was left. In one year we had fewer groups than we had the previous year. After weeks of frustration in trying to salvage what was left of our rapidly dwindling small group ministry, I threw my hands in the air and gave up. I was in Texas with my senior pastor and our care pastor—both men are my best friends as well. I spoke to both of them at different times about what was going on. My senior pastor said something that I had heard before but never applied to my situation. "Healthy things grow." My small group ministry was anything but healthy. Our care pastor reminded me that relationships were key to healthy groups. What I experienced could be compared to building a 4,000 square foot home on a 2,000 square foot foundation. Obviously, everything crumbled. I made some tough decisions. I put everything on hold. I canceled the upcoming church-wide campaign that would have breathed new life into the small group ministry. We canceled all small group connection events. From that moment on, I put all of our focus into one thing—group health. I went to seminars and webinars, read books, listen to podcasts, anything I could do to learn how to build a healthy foundation on which to rebuild the small group ministry. God did not disappoint. Over the next twelve months I was able to adequately develop a support system for our existing groups and slowly began adding new groups. We not only trained new leaders but offered continuing training to all leaders. The reboot allowed us to build a foundation that would provide the support to group leaders that is necessary for building a healthy ministry. Through the long process, I learned several things that are key to healthy groups.

Starting a Group Is Hard

Starting a group is no simple task. In fact, it may be the most difficult part of leading a group. To learn this lesson, I had to launch over a hundred groups and watch them fizzle like a two dollar firework. I was so focused on growth that I neglected health and my neglect had disastrous results. New group leaders desperately need support to get their group off the ground. It is easy to take that for granted and assume that the leaders can handle it with a quick meeting and an encouraging email. Even if a new group does succeed, a lack of support may encourage a group to develop outside the parameters the church is trying to set. But the reality is that most don't even have their first meeting and those that do start barely make it past the first twelve weeks.

A new group needs extra support and attention from the time the group is proposed through the first six to twelve weeks. To have someone walk with a leader through these few weeks is vital to its success. Training meetings, attention to detail, and weekly phone calls are the most basic means of support to a new group leader.

Coaching is Key

Small groups exist, in part, because most churches are too large for one person to manage the spiritual life of everyone in the church. One person, like a senior pastor, cannot effectively minister to a crowd of fifty. Twenty-five? Maybe. Ten? Absolutely. According to a 2015 study, the average church size in the U.S. is seventy-five (Chaves, n.d.)—too many for one person to build deep relationships and experience life on an intimate level. Caring small group leaders in a church of seventy-five lighten that load. The pastor is intimately acquainted with the leaders, meeting their spiritual needs and growing with them. In a church twice that size, there may be too many group leaders for on pastor to relate to. To add a system of coaching is of tremendous importance as a small group ministry grows.

Group coaches are able to serve in two capacities. First, they are the first line of defense and support for group leaders. Coaches are the cheerleaders and mentors to new group leaders. They provide encouragement and support to leaders that have questions or encounter problems within their group. Coaches provide a measure of accountability among group leaders as well, encouraging them to meet a church's expectations for its group leaders.

Coaches also serve in areas of pastoral care. A pastor of even an average sized church will struggle to stay intimately connected with the members of the congregation. It is simply impossible for one person to meet the needs of so many. Small group coaches and group leaders can take the overwhelming burden of pastoral care off of the pastor and lighten that load. Hospital visits, arranging for meals, caring for the sick and elderly within the church can all be accomplished by group coaches and leaders. In Galatians 6:10, Paul says that "we should do well to everyone." He then draws a purposeful distinction—"especially to those of the household of faith." At first glance, this may seem slightly self-serving. But remember what Jesus said:

"Your love for one another will prove to the world that you are my disciples."

John 13:35

Evaluation is Necessary

I've not had many jobs over the years. I'm a pretty loyal employee. The least I've stayed at any one job as an adult is eleven years. I'm going on six at my current place of ministry and have no intention of going anywhere unless God sends me packing. One thing I have learned from the few positions I've held is that employee evaluations are necessary and beneficial to the employee and the employer. I actually look forward to them. I would rather hear an employer say, "you're terrible, and this is what you can do to stop being terrible." It's frustrating when you hear nothing. It's even worse when all I hear is good comments when I know there is room for improvement. I like to know where I stand and what are the expectations that I need to meet. I want to get better at what I do.

If I asked any believer, "Do you want to become a stronger, more committed follower of Jesus?" the answer would always be "yes!" No one would ever claim to be satisfied as a mediocre follower of Jesus that does more sitting than actual following, though that is sadly what many of us do. Deep down, we all have a desire to get better at following Jesus. Simple self-evaluations of one's spiritual walk can satisfy this desire to grow and encourage someone to grow in a particular area. A small group is the best place for this kind of self-evaluation to take place. Whether you are using an assessment tool or a spiritual gifts test, your group members can learn a lot about themselves and their relationship to Jesus. A discussion about everyone's self-evaluation will open the door to discuss the group members' next step or help them set goals to improve weak areas in their lives. You can even set goals for your group and challenge them to improve, encouraging each other toward a particular goal.

My current small group recently took a spiritual health assessment. There are ten of us in the group. We all found that the area of our life that needed the most attention was evangelism. We talked about it and set some simple goals for us to take some steps toward improving our efforts in sharing the gospel. We chose a small group study on evangelism that would give us the tools we need to discuss the gospel story with others. Though our group usually meets at our home, we decided to rotate homes while we did this study and start the evening by walking through our neighborhoods to pray for our neighbors and for ourselves. Finally, we each committed to inviting one neighbor to the next study that we would do as a small group and prayed for our invitees by name. We grew through this process and saw tremendous results among our group. This all happened because we conducted a simple self-evaluation and discussed the results. I now encourage this among all of our groups and include it in our leadership training events.

Spiritually Healthy Leaders Are A Must.

I'm not a small guy. I would benefit by shedding a pound or forty. It doesn't take a skilled diagnostician to make that assessment. Several years ago, I made a visit to a doctor for a physical. It had been a while since seeing a physician so I simply chose a general practitioner that was part of our network and close to home. I went to my appointment and was surprised that he was larger than I was at the time. Not taller or simply a little bigger. This guy easily had me by a hundred pounds or more. He gave me the physical and then made recommendations based on his assessment. His number one recommendation was that I drop twenty-five pounds. My first thought was that I just paid $20 for him to say the same thing my wife told me before I left the house. My second thought was, "you're one to talk, Tubby." Who's this guy telling me to drop a few pounds? I ignored his diagnosis and continued to overeat and avoid exercise at any cost. Two years later, our new insurance company required that I have another physical. I figured I would pay a visit to Dr. Lard Butt. Much to my amazement, the good doctor had shed that hundred pounds and then some. He was the picture of health. I made some smart aleck comment about him being half the man he used to be and then got on with the physical. Again, he made his recommendation to lose twenty-five pounds. Ok, this time it was thirty pounds, but whatever. There was a difference this time. The difference was that he was the picture of health. I could look to him for an example of what my life could be like with a few simple changes.

Now I'm not proposing that it is necessary for you to live a perfect, sin-free life and provide an unrealistic example of what it means to be a follower of Jesus. Besides, we already have that perfect example in Jesus. What I am suggesting is that you, as the leader, model a life that demonstrates honesty and transparency about the transformation taking place in your life. If the point of group life is to experience the transforming power of God together, then transparency is necessary. If the group leader is transparent, all group members will attain at least some level of transparency. On the other hand, if you are hiding your sin for the sake of setting a good example, you are not healthy, nor are you setting a healthy example for the group. This kind of transparency is the first step in developing a culture that seeks spiritual health.

No doubt, the good doctor had a plan to become healthy that included a strict regimen that included diet and exercise. Obviously, he stuck to that plan. As a group leader, you need a plan that encourages spiritual health in your own life. The obvious inclusions to this plan are Bible study, prayer, and being connected to a small group—the same things you tell everyone in your group to do if they want to be spiritually healthy. However, for those things to be most effective, accountability is key.

Once while sitting at a stop light at the intersection of Loxahatchee Drive and Indiantown Road in Jupiter, Florida, I noticed a guy and a girl in workout clothes. That alone is not unusual. What made it odd what that he was carrying her piggyback. Who does this after twelve years of age? Then I noticed another couple a few steps behind them doing the same thing. And another, and another. The next day, I saw other people in workout clothes walking the same road flipping a giant tractor tire as they walked along this busy street. Later I learned that they were members of a gym that apparently specialized in making a fool of grown men and women as well as encouraging health and fitness. I could not help but think that none of these people would put on a pair of yoga pants and do this alone in their front yard. With the right encouragement, people are willing to do whatever it takes to accomplish a goal.

For the same reason, you as a group leader need accountability. You need someone that will encourage you to stay the course and reach your goals spiritually. If you desire to lead a healthy group, start with a healthy leader.

9 CHURCH UNITY BEGINS
IN SMALL GROUPS

*Then make me truly happy by agreeing wholeheartedly
with each other, loving one another, and working
together with one mind and purpose.*
Philippians 2:2

Rehearsal was the best part of being a music teacher. Performance was necessary, but I never looked forward to it. I disliked, as most teachers, the parts of my job that had little to do with teaching—paperwork, car lines, etc. But I loved the rehearsal process. Being able to take forty middle school kids that had limited ability and experience, teach them how to sing and how to read music, and, in time, create music that demonstrated beauty and precision was the most satisfying part of my job. The fact that the forty middle school kids were typically overly self-conscious, even self-absorbed, did not make the job easier. The most important and most difficult part of the task was teaching them to function as one. Before they could experience excellence, they had to experience unity. The pop music icons of the day were examples of self-centeredness and the purpose of their music was to demonstrate the uniqueness of their voice and every middle school girl wanted to sound just like them. This is fine for a soloist, but it does not work in a group.   Not only did they have to learn to sing correctly, they also had to learn to listen.   If they could not or would not hear the voices around them, they could not function as one.   They had to learn how to sing in a way that, at the appropriate time, their part would allow another part to be heard above the rest of the voices.   They had to learn to start and stop every syllable of every word at the same time.   They had to shape the two and three sounds within each single vowel together.   Every breath, inhaled or exhaled, was done in unity.   Unity was necessary for them to function as a single unit that was focused on a single purpose.

Jesus places a high priority on unity in the church.   It is the second to the last thing that Jesus prayed for. In John 17, we hear Jesus pray, "Father, let them be one, as you and I are one."   Then he broadens the scope of this request and says, "not just the twelve that are with me now, but everyone that believes in me because of their message."   Not too many months ago, I read that statement and suddenly felt a pit in my stomach.   Jesus prayed that all believers would experience unity—to be one as God the Father and God the Son are one.   I thought about all the churches I have been associated with over the last three decades and all the pointless stuff that we argued about. Long hair or short hair. Drums or no drums. Skirts or culottes (that one goes way back). The list is long and maddening. I even watched two men shout each other down over which evangelism method was the most biblical.   It is almost as if we spend more time looking for things that divide us rather than experiencing the things that unite us. Maybe it's just me, but I think this breaks the Savior's heart.

How ironic it is to think that we would cause division among ourselves over evangelism methods and philosophies. At the end of John 17, Jesus says, "And may they be in us so that the world will believe you sent me." The unity that Jesus describes is exactly what demonstrates to the world that Jesus is who he says he is—the way, the truth, and the life. According to Jesus, unity is the best evangelism method and essential to a healthy church.

Your small group is the best place to encourage and experience church unity. However, it will not happen by accident. Unity among my choirs never just happened. I had to be intentional. Just as I had to have a plan to create unity among the members of my choirs, a small group leader must have a plan to create unity among small group members.

Many years ago, a former pastor of mine preached a sermon from Philippians 2 that I have never forgotten. His three points were harmony, humility, and helpfulness. To this day, I reference these three points in sermons, marriage counseling, and conflict resolution. In my mind, they sum up the essence of church unity.

Then make me truly happy by agreeing wholeheartedly with each other, loving one another, and working together with one mind and purpose. Don't be selfish; don't try to impress others. Be humble, thinking of others as better than yourselves.

*Don't look out only for your own interests,
but take an interest in others, too.
Philippians 2:2-4*

Harmony

Obviously, the word harmony sums up the goal of working with choirs. It required an intentional effort to make each voice sound as one. Paul calls us to do the same as believers. And that unity will take place as we all work toward, as Paul said, "one mind and purpose." The purpose statement at the church I currently serve is, "Persuading people through love to follow Jesus". We want everyone at Park Valley to do this so we speak of it often. Every group or ministry in our church is expected to make this part of their DNA. We want everyone to be aware of this phrase and make it a part of their personal DNA. Our church is relatively young but has been able to reach thousands of people with the gospel. When we are asked what our secret is, we kind of shrug our shoulders and admit that we do not have the secret formula for church growth, but it is obvious that the phrase, persuading people through love to follow Jesus, has something to do with it. I am privileged to teach our Growth Track classes, a series of classes that assimilate people into the culture of our church. The best part of the class is meeting all the people that are new to the church. We talk with them and take surveys to find out why they came in the first place and why they came back. Nearly every guest says that they were invited by a friend and that the church is friendly. Many go as far as to say they felt like they were at home at Park Valley. No innovative method for church growth—just a church full of people rallying behind a single purpose.

Humility

I had always heard that you could learn humility in the schoolhouse or the woodshed. In other words, you could choose to learn and practice humility of your own accord, or you could choose to learn through humiliation. I chose the woodshed.

I mentioned in a previous chapter that I had studied music at Westminster Choir College. To a musician, this is kind of a big deal. It is a reputable school and I was more than willing to mention to people that I was studying at Westminster. The college is in Princeton, New Jersey, so it was also easy to throw around the name, Princeton, too.

One weekend I had some free time and thought that I would go to downtown Princeton, walk around and get some lunch. It was summer, so I threw on a pair of khaki shorts, a white button-down Izod shirt and a pair of Birkenstock knock-offs. Don't judge me. It was the 90's. I drove the four or five blocks to Nassau Street and parked the car in front of a hip little sidewalk café that served Mexican food with a California flair. I decided to eat there after taking a walk around town to check out all that this part of town had to offer. I crossed the street onto the campus of Princeton University. It was beautiful. I meandered through and around buildings that were tightly fit onto a relatively small piece of property. I found the entrance to the chapel that is on campus and tried to go in, but it was locked, as were most of the buildings. After the University, I walked over to Nassau Presbyterian Church and by luck, the door was open. I walked in and admired the architecture and sat down for a minute or two to get out of the sun.

After walking around for a bit longer. I returned to the café. I walked up to the counter, ordered a burrito, and went to my seat. As I sat at the little table in this open-air café, I began to think about my current situation. In a moment of total arrogance, I thought about how cool it was to be in a town like Princeton, being educated by world-renowned musicians at a school that, at the time, ranked among the best music schools in the world. With all this on my resume, who could resist hiring me? This was my moment. A turning point in my life that would put me on the fast track to a form of significance and celebrity in my little corner of the world.

Welcome to the woodshed.

The server brought me my burrito. It was huge. Without considering the fact that it just came out of a five hundred degree oven, I picked it up and bit into it. This moment was the closest I would ever come to a mouthful of molten lava. I was in extreme pain. Not the, "Oh, that's hot," kind of pain, but the scream like a frightened little girl kind of pain. The whole restaurant turned to look at me as I let out a yell. This was only the beginning of my humiliation. As I bit into the burrito from hell the other end of the burrito had obviously reached its breaking point and exploded. Red sauce and cheese landed on the top half of my white, button-down Izod shirt and oozed its way down like a mudslide. I guzzled my diet coke to cool my flaming tongue. This all happened in a matter of seconds, but it felt like an eternity. And everyone was still watching. I grabbed a napkin and tried to clean it up but only made matters worse. After smearing a mixture of ground beef, refried beans, cheese and red sauce deep into the fibers of my favorite shirt, I decided that it would be better if I cleaned up in the men's room rather than continue being the free entertainment for the other diners. I walked to the restroom only to be greeted by a handwritten out of order sign. I headed toward the counter. The cashier looked at me like I was the victim of a violent crime. I asked her if there was another restroom nearby. She looked at me compassionately and pointed. "There's a public restroom down the street about three blocks."

I walked the humiliating three blocks ignoring the obvious stares and pretending that nothing was wrong. I found the men's room and went in. Water and brown paper towels did little more than set the stain. At least the thick layer of refried beans was gone.

I was in a men's room, so I took advantage of my situation and did what you are supposed to do in a men's room. When I went to zip up, you guessed it, my zipper broke. In the down position, of course. I rolled my eyes and headed to the door. As I exited, my right faux Birkenstock caught the threshold of the doorway and ripped loose from the soul of the sandal.

The next three blocks were agonizing. I felt the pitiful stare of everyone that happened to look my way. I tried to walk quickly but was obviously handicapped by the flopping sandal and the awkward way I held the tail of my now red, brown, and white shirt in front of my broken zipper. When I stopped at a crosswalk, a nice lady sympathetically asked if I was okay. My tongue still hurt and felt like it was three times its normal size in my mouth, so I kept my reply short. "Yeth. Thank you."

I walked the final two blocks to my car. Stuck to the windshield was a parking ticket for ten dollars. I held it in the air and looked up to the heavens. "Funny. Real funny," I said to the creator of the heavens and earth. I knew exactly the lesson I was supposed to learn in that moment.

> *"Don't be selfish. Don't try to impress others. Be humble."*

I violated all three of Paul's imperatives and God responded accordingly. James could not have been clearer when he said that God resists the proud but gives grace to the humble. The only grace I experienced that day was when I thanked God for the burrito. When I chose arrogance, I chose the woodshed.

Helpfulness

The Church at Philippi was a healthy church. As Paul addressed the churches in his letter, he would always say why he was thankful for them. Too many of the churches, he would explain why they needed his attention. He was shocked that the Galatians were turning from God in such a short period of time. He told the Romans that they were in no position to judge sinners. The Ephesian believers were experiencing division from their Jewish brothers and sisters. The church at Philippi was different.

Paul praised them for their love for each other. He thanked them for supporting him in his work. His desire for them was that they learn to love each other more than they already were.

In chapter four of his letter to the Philippian Church, we find one of Paul's most quoted verses. We claim this verse when facing insurmountable odds. When we are being stretched beyond our emotional and spiritual limits we cry out, "I can do all things through Christ who gives me strength!" And we can. But we ignore the surrounding verses. Early in the letter, Paul had thanked them for helping him in times of struggle. Prior to the familiar statement, he said that he had learned to exist under the most difficult circumstances with only the bare necessities on which to survive because, he could do "all things through Christ," but look at the following verses.

Even so, you have done well to share with me in my present difficulty. As you know, you Philippians were the only ones who gave me financial help when I first brought you the Good News and then traveled on from Macedonia. No other church did this. Even when I was in Thessalonica you sent help more than once. I don't say this because I want a gift from you. Rather, I want you to receive a reward for your kindness.
Philippians 4:14-17

What set the Philippians apart from the other churches? Helpfulness. Yes, Paul could do all things through Jesus, but God chose to use the help of fellow believers while he was in the toughest of circumstances. They prayed for him and provided for his needs. When he was with them, they made sure he had the funds to continue spreading the gospel.

In Philippians 2:5, Paul sums up these three thoughts—harmony, humility, and helpfulness—with a phrase that is key to church unity.

You must have the same attitude that
Christ Jesus had.

Imagine a church full of people that sought to think the way Jesus does. The following verses are, in my opinion, the best description of Jesus' attitude. They are a very concise snapshot into the mind of Christ.

Though he was God, he did not think of equality with
God as something to cling to. Instead, he gave up
his divine privileges; he took the humble position of
a slave and was born as a human being.
When he appeared in human form, he humbled
himself in obedience to God and died a criminal's
death on a cross.

Philippians 2:6-8

Simply put, Jesus' example was to submit, serve, and sacrifice.

Submit

I can't imagine a greater act of submission than to temporarily set aside your position as Lord and Savior to live as a man on earth, knowing that your life would end in homelessness, persecution, and an agonizing criminal's death. Jesus did this willingly. He had an out. He could have called the armies of heaven to rescue him at any moment. But he willingly submitted to God's plan. If we live by his example and submit to God's plan we will experience the harmony that results from "working together with one mind and purpose."

I once heard a pastor refer to the word submit as the "S" word because it is an often avoided topic. When we hear the word submit, our minds may turn immediately to Ephesians 5 where wives are told to submit to their husbands. We think of submission as a point two in a sermon on marriage. But right before Paul reminds wives to submit to their husbands, he says this:

> *And further, submit to one another out of reverence for Christ.*
>
> Ephesians 5:21

Biblical submission is more than submitting to God. It begins but does not end there. Just before reminding wives that they are to practice the "S" word toward their husbands, Paul says that we are to submit to each other out of reverence for Jesus. Real submission begins with humility. It is easy to say that we submit to God—he's God. He's all-knowing, all-powerful, all-present. When Job questioned his situation, God's answer began with, "Where were you when I hung the sun, moon, and stars in the sky?" We will all admit to submitting to God, the creator and sustainer of all things. Submitting to each other is altogether different, requiring a humility that comes completely through Christ living in us.

Paul continues his letter by discussing relationships. At the end of chapter five, he discusses the relationships between husbands and wives. In chapter six, he discusses parents and children and slaves and masters. Each of these relationships requires a measure of humility that does not come naturally.

We are selfish by nature. A child's first words may be mama or dada, but somewhere on the list of top ten words for infants is usually "no" or "mine!" We may teach them the actual words, but we do not have to teach them motivation for those words. We go through life and learn to share and say I'm sorry. We learn to treat others the way we want to be treated but in the end, we are still selfish. Getting married proves it. Think about it. When someone is considering marriage they are looking for someone who meets MY needs. Someone who completes ME. Someone who loves ME unconditionally. No one says, "I want to marry the wretched refuse of society so that I can lavish them with unconditional love". Why, because we are innately selfish. A love for and humility toward others comes from a changed heart that seeks to glorify the Savior.

Serve

I have repeatedly mentioned my ineptness as a gardener. I try. I really do. I read books. I take notes. I really want to be a good, no, a great gardener. God would just rather that I get lots of sermon illustrations from the experience. But I do know one thing for sure: if the plant isn't producing fruit, it's not healthy. The Bible tells us that serving will cause us to be mature fruit-bearers.
In Ephesians 4, Paul discusses church unity. In verses 11 and 12 he tells us that God has provided

us with people that possess certain gifts for the purpose of equipping God's people to "*do his work*," and "*build up the church.*" The following verses explain to us what unity looks like in the church.

> *This* [leaders equipping people to build the church] *will continue until we all come to such unity in our faith and knowledge of God's Son that we will be mature in the Lord, measuring up to the full and complete standard of Christ. Then we will no longer be immature like children. We won't be tossed and blown about by every wind of new teaching. We will not be influenced when people try to trick us with lies so clever they sound like the truth. Instead, we will speak the truth in love, growing in every way more and more like Christ, who is the head of his body, the church. He makes the whole body fit together perfectly. As each part does its own special work, it helps the other parts grow, so that the whole body is healthy and growing and full of love.*
>
> Ephesians 4:13-16

As believers are equipped to build the church we experience unity, acquire an intimate knowledge of Jesus, and become more like him. You cannot become like Jesus apart from serving. If our growing as a believer means becoming more like Jesus, then we must serve. Additionally, serving has an impact on the entire body of believers. This is made clear in the last two sentences of the passage. He makes each part fit together perfectly and as each person serves in his or her own unique way produces growth in others so that the church is "healthy, growing and full of love." A church full of servants is a church that experiences unity.

I am grateful for every servant in every church that I've had the privilege of serving. They are the ones that truly bring joy to ministry. However, serving Biblically requires more than signing up and showing up. Consider Paul's description of Jesus as a servant in Philippians 2.

Instead, he gave up his divine privilege; he took the humble position of a slave...

Philippians 2:7

Some translations say servant. Some say slave. The literal meaning of the word is slave. There is a difference between a servant and a slave. A servant can expect something in return for his service. A true servant, a servant like Jesus, serves expecting nothing in return. He simply responds to the Word of God and serves.

Church Unity and Your Small Group

Group leaders are in a special position to promote unity in their small groups. If you want to be intentional about promoting church unity, implement these practices in your group.

Practice Accountability

Accountability is a frightening concept to most. But to those that have experienced it, it is a vital part of their growth as a believer. What makes it frightening is that we have to submit ourselves to someone else in order to get another perspective on how we need to submit to God. In the small group setting, there is a natural measure of accountability.

We talk to some extent about what we struggle with. The discussion could always dig a little deeper, but there is at least a small amount of accountability. Without an intentional effort to facilitate a more intimate level of accountability, it will never happen. Utilizing a spiritual health assessment tool is a good way to begin the process of creating effective accountability. Encouraging group members to identify spiritual shortcomings in their lives and to take their next step is accountability. Once your group members are used to these conversations, encourage them to partner up to hold each other accountable.

Encourage Members to Serve

We've already established that serving creates unity and spiritual growth. It is an essential component of discipleship. If, as a leader, you are encouraging spiritual growth, then by default you should be encouraging service. If there are people in your group that are not serving then encourage them to serve. Plan to do a study on serving and discuss the benefits of serving to both the individual and to the church. Invite them to serve with you or plan to serve at an event as a group. If your church has an opportunity for members to discover spiritual gifts, encourage your group members to participate. If not, then do a small group study on spiritual gifts and encourage members to choose a place to serve based on their giftedness.

Speak Positively About Your Church

I've had the privilege to speak to a handful of pastors about changing from a Sunday school model to a small group model. I hear many of the same questions in each situation, but the one question I hear more than any other is,

"How do you prevent a group of people from bad-mouthing the church and leading people away?"

Pastors fear the devastation of division in their churches and the idea of turning people lose to meet on their own time in their own space sounds dangerous—especially if a pastor has experienced division in the past. This is a legitimate and common fear.

A small group that is intentional about promoting church unity will put a pastor's fear to rest. As a group leader, always speak positively about your church. Your group leaders respect you, otherwise, they would not be a part of your group, and will respect your opinion of the church and its leaders. If you speak positively, they are more likely to speak positively as well.

Squash Gossip

No, your church leaders are not perfect. They will make mistakes and people will want to talk about them. It should be understood by everyone in your group that there is no place for gossip. When gossip occurs, and it will, the group leader should quietly and gently address the problem of gossip.

Pray for Your Church And Its Leaders

I'm kind of a sci-fi geek. My greatest self-indulgence is that I want to own all of the Marvel movies on

DVD. I've watched both complete Star Wars trilogies dozens of times. There are many common themes in science fiction movies. One constant theme is, *it's never a good idea to disconnect from the mothership*. When you do, you've lost communication and protection. You're on your own. A small group that prays for its church and its leaders maintains a strong connection to "the mothership". Praying for the church will focus your group on the mission of the church. Praying for events, ministries and, of course, people will keep your group focused on the common purpose of your church. Praying for pastors and church leaders will create a connection between leaders and group members that help to develop a strong sense of unity. Conversely, a group that does not pray for its church and her leaders remains disconnected from the common purpose. The focus can quickly turn inward to selfish needs and desires.

As a group leader, be intentional about focusing your group on the church during prayer time. Be aware of upcoming church events that could potentially impact the community or spread the gospel around the world. Encourage your group to pray for the events and then follow up with reports of what happened at the event. Talk about lives that were changed, people that were saved, and victories that were won. Take the time to thank and praise God in prayer for what God accomplished through your church. Also, make your group aware of the personal needs of your pastors and church leaders. Knowing that a pastor or leader has the same physical, emotional, and spiritual problems as everyone else creates an unexpected connection between them and the person in the pew. As your group prays for these leaders, take a moment to send the leader a card signed by everyone in your group and let them know that you are praying for them.

A Final Word on Unity

Before Jesus, who prayed for unity in his final hours on earth, ascended to heaven, he left the disciples with a mission—a purpose. When Paul spoke of unity in Philippians 2, he also spoke of having the same mind and purpose. Peter also spoke of our purpose in Christ and emphasized unity. If our purpose as believers is so closely connected to unity in the words of Jesus, Paul and Peter, then it makes sense that an intentional focus on the stated purpose of your church within your group would promote church unity among your group members. As the leader, always lead toward unity with your church, never away. Be your church's biggest cheerleader for the sake of accomplishing a common purpose.

10 GOD DESERVES IT, THAT'S WHY

He has given me a new song to sing,
a hymn of praise to our God.
Many will see what he has done and be amazed.
They will put their trust in the Lord.
Psalm 40:3

Before my dad built houses, he worked in an electronics store in Arlington, Virginia. I was young and barely remember it, but I do remember that there were some cool electronic gadgets around the house for a long time after he stopped working there. One such device was an old reel to reel tape recorder and player. We did not use it much when I was young except to play the old reel to reel tapes that the family had made before I was born. There were tapes of old sermons, sounds of Christmas morning, and kids being silly. One of my favorite things to hear was some of the oldest tapes of our extended family gathering on the front porch of Aunt Lizzie's house with guitars, banjos, and mandolins, singing old hymns. The sound was joyous and festive. Everyone sang along. There was always four-part harmony and no one seemed to be self-conscious about singing in public. Music was a natural pastime. In that day, standing around the piano and singing was not uncommon. It was a part of life. Corporate singing was a staple of the culture.

That was then. Fast forward to the present. When is the last time you got together with a group of friends just to sing? My kids are musical. They sing and play instruments but not once did I see them get together with their friends for the sole purpose of singing. Oddly enough, however, when we think of worship in a small group, our minds immediately land on images of a circle of people, one of whom plays guitar, eyes closed, hands in the air, singing worships songs. If your group does that, awesome. You are certainly among the minority. No doubt those worshipful moments add a tremendous amount of depth to the relationships you have developed with God and the other people in your small group. Most group leaders, however, feel inadequate when it comes to leading others in worship and not every group is blessed with a guitar player.

A spiritual turning point in my life came in my early thirties. I was still teaching music and serving part-time at a church working with children and helping in the worship ministry. I was young and arrogant. I considered myself to be above the musical standard set by most churches. I boastfully swore that I would never be a church musician. God had different plans. In spite of my arrogance, I sought a truly worshipful experience that I was not finding in church. I read and researched. My shelves were full of books on worship, none of which were satisfying my desire to know God more.

Every November, I would take a group of young musicians to a choral festival at Stetson University in DeLand, Florida. While the kids rehearsed, I would take the time to visit the bookstore. On one of my stops, I came across a book from an author I had never heard of. The title of the book caught my eye. It was called, A Royal Waste of Time: The Splendor of Worshiping God and Being Church for the World. I opened to the introduction and started reading. What I read hit me between my sanctimonious eyes and totally changed the way I think about worship. Marva Dawn, the author of this great book, writes:

> To worship the Lord is—in the world's eyes—a waste of time. It is, indeed, a royal waste of time, but a waste nonetheless. By engaging in it, we don't accomplish anything useful in our society's terms.
>
> "Worship ought not to be construed in a utilitarian way. Its purpose is not to gain numbers nor for our churches to be seen as successful. Rather, the entire reason for our worship is that God deserves it. Moreover, it isn't even useful for earning points with God, for what we do in worship won't change one whit how God feels about us. We will always still be helpless sinners caught in our endless inability to be what we should or to make ourselves better—and God will always be merciful, compassionate, and gracious, abounding in steadfast love and ready to forgive us as we come to him." (Dawn, 1999)

It was as if I had walked out of a dark room and

seen clearly for the first time. I had been a musician my entire adult life and many years before that. I had sung in and lead church choirs. I traveled and sang with a gospel quartet. I taught music in schools and in private studios. Yet, somehow I missed the point when it comes to worshiping the God of the universe. Worship, as Ms. Dawn wrote, exists because God deserves it. I waited for the worship experience. I wanted the hairs to rise on the back of my neck and feel the spirit wind across my face. I wanted my efforts to wow a crowd. The only thing I was worshipping was my own selfish desires and snobbish musical standards. In that moment I realized that the end result of worship is simply to worship. I bought the book.

The next few years, God changed my heart and mind concerning worship. I realized, over time, that worship was not about music. Worship includes any medium that is used to ascribe worth to God. The painter worships God on his canvas. The sculpture in his clay. The photographer through his lens. But even those examples imply unnecessary limits. Colossians 3:17 reminds us to "*do all to the glory of God.*"

Worship is a performance only to those who perform. To the rest of us, worship is about ascribing worth to God in our everyday lives. One of the best things your group can do to worship is to simply talk about God. Psalm 29 is a perfect example. Yes, it was intended to be sung, but look at David's beautiful lyrics.

Honor the Lord, you heavenly beings;
honor the Lord for his glory and strength.

Honor the Lord for the glory of his name.
Worship the Lord in the splendor of his holiness.
The voice of the Lord echoes above the sea.
The God of glory thunders.
The Lord thunders over the mighty sea.
The voice of the Lord is powerful;
the voice of the Lord is majestic.
The voice of the Lord splits the mighty cedars;
the Lord shatters the cedars of Lebanon.
He makes Lebanon's mountains skip like a calf;
he makes Mount Hermon leap like a young wild
ox.
The voice of the Lord strikes
with bolts of lightning.
The voice of the Lord makes the barren wilderness
quake;
the Lord shakes the wilderness of Kadesh.
The voice of the Lord twists mighty oaks
and strips the forests bare.
In his Temple everyone shouts, "Glory!"
The Lord rules over the floodwaters.
The Lord reigns as king forever.
The Lord gives his people strength.
The Lord blesses them with peace.

Maybe it's just me, but if it were about the music, God would have preserved a musical score to accompany this Psalm. Instead, he simply preserved the words to the cry of David's heart—a testament to God's mighty power. In his commentary, Matthew Henry supposes that David was an eyewitness to a terrible storm that demonstrated the awesome power of God through his creation. (Henry, n.d.) Similarly, in Psalm 8, David references the vastness of God as he stares into the night sky. In other Psalms, David speaks of God's comfort and protection when he was alone and on the run from an angry King. He praised God for the victories he experienced in literal battles and personal conflict. David simply spoke of the presence of God in his life. No matter the circumstances, David's words of praise answered the question, "What is God doing in your life today?"

Worship in your small group can be as simple as that—talking about God's presence in your life. An intentional effort on the part of a group leader to lead others in this kind of discussion can be a game changer for your group. Talking about a curriculum is one thing. Talking about God's presence in everyday life is altogether different and life-changing. Many do not see the presence of God in their lives until someone else points it out. Affirming God's presence in your life or the life of one of your members strengthens faith and trust in God.

Not too long after the Israelites left Egypt, Moses' father in law, Jethro, traveled from Midian to greet him. Moses told them of all that God had done to deliver Israel. He spoke of the hardening of Pharaoh's heart, the plagues, and the burning bush. He told them of their escape and the defeat of the Egyptian army at the hand of God. Upon hearing this, Jethro said,

> *I know now that the Lord is greater than all other gods, because he rescued his people from the oppression of the proud Egyptians."* Exodus 18:11

We do not know who Jethro worshipped before this moment. It is clear that at that moment, Jethro's faith was strengthened upon hearing the greatness of God in the life of his son in law and his people. Small group meetings are the perfect setting to affirm the presence of God in the life of a believer. There are three ways this is most often accomplished.

Affirming God's Presence through Prayer

It goes without saying that prayer should be an important part of your group meeting. It is necessary for people to share their needs and struggles so that the body of Christ can support them in prayer. However, when prayer is that and nothing more, we are missing a great opportunity. Not only should we be "making our requests know unto him," we need to affirm God's presence in the life of a group member as they ask the group to pray for them. As people share the intimate circumstances of their past and present, there exists an opportunity to point out how God may have worked through those challenging times. Group members will undoubtedly begin to see the hand of God on their lives during times when perhaps it felt as if God was nowhere to be found.

Affirming God's Presence through Intentional Praise

The brief question, "Any prayer request?" is inevitably followed by, "Any praises?" As leaders, we all tend to wrap up that last few minutes of group time with these two inquiries. There is absolutely nothing wrong with this. Our intentions are good, and the opportunity to share the details of our week is healthy. But simply asking these questions can also be limiting. Yes, we should be praising God for the good things he has done since the last group meeting and we should be sharing the answers to our prayers, giving God the glory. A group leader that is more intentional in guiding his group through a time of praise will create opportunities for group members to not only recognize how God is meeting their needs, but also to praise God for who he is.

I once had a youth pastor that was a master at this. At least, as a seventh grader, I thought he was a master. Maybe they taught him this stuff on his first day at youth pastor school. At the end of nearly every youth event, whether it be bowling, skating, or blindly grabbing something out of a brown shopping bag, Brother Rick, as we called him, always ended the night with a time in the word. I remember many of those times including unique ways to worship God. Of course, we sang. But Rick afforded us the opportunity to describe God in creative ways. One sentence explanations of how God was transforming our lives. Single-word statements that completed the phrase, "My God is..." Saying a one-sentence prayer that began, "Thank you God for..." It made us think beyond the obvious. It made us concentrate on an all-powerful, ever-present God that deserved to be publicly worshipped. Incorporating similar opportunities with your group will, no doubt, warrant the same results.

Affirming God's Presence through Group Discussion

I love the discussion time. The videos are great. The fellowship time is awesome. But the discussion is the best part, in my opinion, of the group meeting. It is during this time that you get to know your group members better and find out what motivates them, scares them, or what makes them laugh. I believe very strongly that the greatest potential for growth and transformation among the members of a group takes place during this time. A big reason for this is that we, at least in this setting, are inclined to affirm God's presence in the life of someone else. I cannot begin to guess the number of times in group meetings over the years, someone will mention a particular struggle and someone else will say, "I've been through the exact same thing!" Whether it is health issues, marriage and family struggles, job changes, or whatever God seems intentional about bringing people together that share nearly identical experiences.

In a recent group meeting, one of the moms in the group was sharing her fear of a potential medical procedure on her young son—not just any procedure but a kind of rare and somewhat drastic procedure used in both cancer and sickle cell treatments. As if scripted, one of the other moms said, my son received the same treatment several years ago. Just knowing that God cared enough to bring someone into that discussion that could say, "here is what God did for us under the same circumstances," is more than enough to confirm that God cares about the situation and is going to walk that path with you. As a leader in the group, it is important to be intentional in identifying those connections between group members.

The consequences of one's actions is another valuable affirmation of God's presence that often comes up during discussions. It is easy to talk about the times when God shows up like a knight on a white horse and saves the day with miraculous healings and awe-inspiring answers to the cry of our hearts. It is another thing altogether to speak candidly about the times God showed up to kick butt and take names. There are often significant consequences to our sinful choices. We have all experienced them. To openly discuss, or encourage others to discuss, the consequences of our past indiscretions may be exactly what a group member needs to hear to avoid the same mistakes. Again, a group leader that is intentional about affirming God's presence in the lives of group members, will gently and with great discretion, take advantage of these opportunities.

Practical Ways To Worship With Your Group

I've spent a good amount of ink making the point that worship is not simply about music, but we would all agree that it is most people's favorite form of worship, whether we are participating or not. We may differ in our choice of musical style, but we all instinctively think music when we think of worship. Being a musician, or at least a former musician, I think that perhaps God intended it to be that way. So naturally, we cannot have a discussion on worship in your group without discussing music.

We don't have to be performers or even have performers in our group, in order to use music for group worship. There are a number of ways to incorporate music into your group time. The simplest and perhaps the most effective is to simply play worship music as people are entering your home. Music is powerful. Trumpets brought down the walls of Jericho. David's harp soothed Saul's troubled spirit. King Jehoshaphat put singers on the front lines to defeat the armies of three nations. If the music of God can achieve such great things, simply playing worship music could have a profound impact on your group time. It may simply set the tone for the evening, or it may be life-changing to someone that needs that song at that time. In my own experience, there is a song associated with each of three major life changes over the past thirty years. (Thank you DC Talk, John Rutter, and Bobby Michaels for your ministry of music.)

If worshipping with music feels uncomfortable among your group members, there are always opportunities to participate together in corporate worship outside of group time. Obviously, you can attend church together, sit together as a group and experience the joy of worship as a group amid a crowd of believers. Christian concerts also afford your group the opportunity to experience worship together. Opportunities outside of normally scheduled group meetings are also necessary for building those close relationships.

The Last Word On Worship

If I knew I only had a limited amount of time left on this earth, I would have much to say to my children. Though I have spent a lifetime teaching them about life and love and the God that created and redeemed them, I often feel as though there is still so much that I desperately need to say to them. How could I ever condense that down into a brief discussion that would prepare them for the adventures that lie ahead? In the final days of the Old Testament period, God spoke his last words to the children of Israel through the prophet Malachi. Though Malachi contains strong reprimands to priests, and definitive statements on marriage, finances, and more, it is ultimately a book on worship.

"I have loved you."

God's opening statement to this final discussion says more than one might immediately notice.

"I have loved you..." even though you disobeyed me in the garden.
"I have loved you..." even though I could only find eight people worthy of redemption before the flood.
"I have loved you..." even when you turned your back on me after I made you a prosperous nation.
"I have loved you..." even though you wanted to return to slavery after I delivered you.

Those statements only represent the first two books of the Old Testament. We could continue these statements on page after page. Nevertheless, God continued to love his chosen people. He desired their worship as a parent craves the love of a wandering child.

I wish one of you would shut the temple doors, so you would no longer kindle a useless fire on My altar! I am not pleased with you," says the LORD of Hosts, "and I will accept no offering from your hands."
Malachi 1:10 (HCSB)

Very strong words from a very disappointed God. He is speaking to the priests—those responsible for the spiritual well-being of the people he loves dearly. Throughout the book, he chides them for their "useless fire"—offering sacrifices, yet not honoring him in other important areas of their lives.

You worship, but you don't offer God your best. (Malachi 1:6-14)

You worship, but you are not faithful in marriage. (Malachi 2:13-15)

You worship, but you are dishonest with the money that I bless you with. (Malachi 3:6-12)

You worship, but you complain about God's provision. (Malachi 3:14)

Worship is more than music. It is more than mere words at an appropriate time. The common perspective on worship is that we worship God because he did something awesome when we obeyed him. I think that it is time we turn the tables in our small groups and encourage our members to obey God because he is worthy of our worship. He deserves it.

11 PLANNING EACH MEETING

Always plan ahead. It wasn't raining when Noah built the ark. Richard Cushing

When I began my first full-time job as a music teacher in Jupiter, Florida, I was given the unexpected task of teaching music to four-year-olds. I had not hung out with four-year-olds since I was four-years-old. But, I had a college degree and a generous helping of overconfidence. What could possibly go wrong?

I started the year by working on a school-wide music program for which I was given a little more than a month to prepare. I was told the program was to be patriotic themed, involve all 250 students from four year old kindergarten to grade twelve, and be no more than twenty minutes in length. Because the entire first six weeks of all my classes were devoted to this program, I knew there was little room for actual teaching. For the first couple of weeks, all I needed to do was put the words of the songs on the chalkboard and help the kids memorize the music and lyrics.

The four-year-old kindergarten class entered the room around 10:30 a.m.—my very first class as a professional teacher. They walked into the room in a straight line. It was very straight because they had practiced walking in a line all morning. I gave them simple instructions.

"Go clockwise around the circle and stop at the last chair then take your seat."

Confused, they entered the room. The line soon disassembled into a slow-moving mass of frightened toddlers.

"No, this way. THIS way." I motioned, pointing them in the correct direction. "All the way to the last chair."

The line loosely recreated itself as the kids moved around the outside of the circle of chairs. "Inside the circle. No, this way. Inside the chairs."

They circled completely around the outside of the chairs. I took the hand of the line leader who was now more lost and frightened than before. I lead her to the inside of the circle and scooted her in the right direction assuming everyone would follow. With some coaxing they all did.

"All the way to the last chair."

It was a circle. There is no last chair. At least not in the mind of a four-year-old. If I had left the room at that moment, I believe with all my heart they would still be there, twenty-eight years later, walking in that circle looking for the last chair.

I finally got the line leader to stop at what I knew was the last chair. I thought the rest of the kids would understand that they were to take their place in each subsequent chair behind the leader. Not that day. They all kept coming toward the last chair, occupied by the line leader, who was now in tears. They pushed and shoved and fought to sit in the last chair. Obviously frustrated, I led them, one by one to their own chair and was ready to begin my lesson.

I introduced myself and attempted to play a short game with them in a desperate effort to regain their focus. Again, they did not get the directions. The game was a flop. I was exhausted and ready for this thirty-minute class to be over. I still had twenty-eight minutes to go.

I jumped right into teaching them the songs for the twenty-minute patriotic extravaganza. I called their attention to the lyrics neatly written on the chalkboard, instructed them to recite the words along with me, and pointed to the first line. I began reading. Alone. I looked at the kids. They sat silent and a little confused. I was then reminded by one astute child that they were, in fact, four years old and could not read. We played Simon Says for the final twenty-seven minutes. When their teacher returned, she asked how things went. "Awesome!" I replied. She didn't believe me for a second. I told the kids to line up. By then, they had forgotten how to make a line.

I made two mistakes that day. I failed to plan appropriately for that particular day and I did not anticipate what could go wrong. Though your small group meetings may never include a horde of clueless four-year-olds, a simple plan and consideration of potential calamity will prevent the adult version of the confusion of my first day of teaching.

Make It Simple

Life is complicated enough. No one needs more to do that takes up precious time. Keeping your meetings simple will make your meetings a breath of fresh air. Complicated expectations can make group feel more like an obligation than something everyone looks forward to. I personally have a no homework policy in my groups. Many of the studies have a homework option that members may complete if they are so inclined. Unless it is part of church-wide emphasis, we do not do homework. In two decades of ministry, no one has complained. Many have said thank you. Keeping things simple for the group is a priority of mine. Spiritual growth is not contingent on completing daily assignments.

Having a simple agenda will also help you to keep the evening simple. It does not need to be a complicated lesson plan complete with learning outcomes and standard achievement objectives. A simple outline of what is happening that night will eliminate guesswork, keep you on time, and maintain the focus of the evening.

Make It Social

In chapter six of this book, we discussed the particulars of having a plan to be social. Our focus then was on specific events apart from the normal group study for the purpose of deepening relationships. On the other hand, having a simple plan to be intentionally social in each meeting is equally important. It is an opportunity for your guests to take a deep breath, relax, and settle into an intimate experience. Serving a snack and a beverage is always a win. When everyone contributes, it makes for light conversation about the group members' latest culinary conquest. Everyone is grateful and well-fed.

Part of creating a relaxed social atmosphere at group involves taking away potential faux pas that make for an awkward moment. Forgetting names is not uncommon and forgivable during the first few meetings. After several meetings, name forgetting is downright unforgivable. This is more likely to happen if you meet bi-weekly or monthly, but I have made this mistake after many months of meeting weekly with the same people. Sorry, Bob. A simple way to remedy this is with a simple name tag. You will obviously cease using these after some time, but it is always a good idea to have when new people are added to the group. Having a few on hand is never a bad idea. As the leader of the group, you can also make it a priority to know everyone's name well and use them often in group time. As other people hear you, they are reminded of everyone's name and the awkward moment is avoided.

Creating a social atmosphere in your group meetings does not require hours of planning and research, but it does require some intentional effort on your part. A simple google search for icebreakers or games will produce more results than you could use in a lifetime. Selecting a few ahead of time for the purpose of helping your group get to know each other more is worth the little time and effort it will take.

Make it Strategic

Planning your group meeting is not rocket science. Creating a strategy for each meeting is not a difficult task and should not take much time. Failing to have a simple strategy for each meeting will rarely end in disaster but could create awkward or embarrassing moments. By asking yourself a few simple questions, you can develop a simple plan to use for your group meetings.

Are children welcome?

If you are inviting young parents to your group, you must have a plan for their kids. The plan could be that each family takes care of their own childcare or that you may work together to provide childcare during group. Regardless, you must have a plan.

Who is responsible for what?

Sharing the responsibility of the group makes your job easier and causes a sense of ownership among group members. It is important that you communicate these responsibilities to your group members.

How long should we chat and eat before the Bible study begins?

I learned from experience that if you do not put even

a loose limit on the fellowship time in your group, it can easily get out of control. Simply stating as part of your plan that there will be twenty minutes of fellowship before the Bible study begins will help to create a smooth transition between the two. Everyone expects it, so no one is offended when you politely interrupt a conversation to begin the Bible study.

How long is the Bible study going to last?

Helping people to apply the Bible to their everyday lives is obviously why you are leading a small group and it is ultimately why people join small groups. Therefore, this part of the evening will generally take up the larger part of your time together. But prayer is equally important when it comes to the application of God's word to everyday life. Think about James 5:16 again.

Confess your sins to each other and pray for each other so that you may be healed. The earnest prayer of a righteous person has great power and produces wonderful results.

Talk about sin. Talk about your faults and failures. Talk about the effects of living in a fallen world. But the real power of transformation comes through prayer.

Pray for each other so that you may be healed.

There is power in prayer. Cramming a brief prayer time in at the end of a lesson could be considered powerless. Plan a time limit on your Bible study so that you have ample time to pray together. Your group needs this powerful time together.

How long is the prayer time going to last?

Knowing that prayer has the power to transform the members of your group, take into consideration how much time you are going to spend in prayer together. Selecting a general length of time for prayer and sticking to it is good practice and promotes prayer within your group. Without a plan, you are more likely to neglect prayer.

Flexibility is key to part of any plan, especially when it comes to prayer. Some of the most pivotal points in a person's life happen at that moment when they are surrounded by others in prayer.

Recently, we did a study on the Holy Spirit. In this study, we were challenged to do something we knew we were supposed to do but were afraid to. It was a challenge to us all, but one woman, in particular, had a situation that would be extremely difficult. Because we knew her well, we all knew the specifics of her story. She had been estranged from her brother for over twenty years. Though both of them grew up in a Christian home, they both chose very different paths. She chose to follow Jesus and a life of obedience to God's word. Her brother, in response to a painful childhood, chose a life characterized by addiction, homelessness, and prison. She responded to the challenge to follow the Holy Spirit and do what frightened her. Through tears, she committed to reaching out to her brother to seek forgiveness and reconciliation. We dropped everything. The ladies in the group instinctively surrounded her and prayed for her. This pivotal moment started a chain of events that only a loving God could set into place. We continued to pray for her and her brother for weeks as the story of redemption unfolded before our eyes. Soon, they reconnected and renewed not only their relationship but relationships with other family members as well. The brother gave his life to Christ and she was able to surprise her brother and attend his baptism. They now communicate daily. God is doing an amazing transformation in both their lives. Though we may never know this side of heaven, it is possible that had we neglected that time of prayer, this amazing story may have never happened.

Include intentional prayer in your plan for each group meeting. Consider what your group members may be going through. They may need that extra time knowing that others are praying for them.

CONCLUSION

*You can't plow a field simply by
turning it over in your mind.
Gordon B. Hinckley*

James, the brother of Jesus, is abundantly clear that the Bible is less about learning and more about doing. Though I would never even begin to compare the value of this book to the pricelessness of scriptural truth, the principle of James 1:22 most definitely applies. Not because you have read the end all, be all of Small Group how-to books but because merely knowing is not enough to make any improvements or changes to your group. You must take the initiative. You must be intentional. Whether you need a total reboot or simple improvements to your group, start by following these steps.

Evaluate Your Group

Ask yourself some tough questions. If the purpose of discipleship is to become more like Jesus, honestly determine if that kind of transformation is taking place in your group. Are people changing their habits or healing their hurts. Are they serving more, loving more, or being more generous. If nothing has changed over time, then perhaps other changes need to take place. More Bible study. Less Bible study and more prayer. New people. New challenges. When things cease to grow, they are not healthy and need some attention. Take time to make an assessment of what God is doing in your group and consider the transformation taking please in your life and your group members'.

Talk To Your Group

If there is a deficiency of anything in your group, your group members will know. They will know what they need most. They are the ones that know your group routine and people as much as you. Talk to them and learn from the discussion. You may find that they have the pulse on the heartbeat of the group more than you do.

Make a List of Changes That Need to Be Made

There is an old Southern saying that says, "Worry about the alligator closest to the boat." In other words, take care of the urgent first. As you make your list of changes to your group, note the changes that you can implement immediately. You may not be able to change locations immediately, but you could change the time of day if that is what is most affecting the group. If you can change it now, don't wait. Ecclesiastes 11: for says, "Farmers who wait for perfect whether never plant." Don't be a perfectionist farmer when it comes to your group. If a change needs to take place and there is nothing to prevent you, then make the change.

Every journey starts with one step. As you close this book you will be tempted to place it in the bookcase and move on to the next book. Books are not meant to be trophies on a shelf. Books are meant to change us. Take a moment now to ask yourself the tough questions about your group and about yourself as a leader. Don't wait. Make one change before this book begins to collect dust.

ABOUT THE AUTHOR

John Mozingo is the Next Step Pastor at Park Valley Church in Haymarket, Virginia. He has served for many years as both an educator and pastor in music and discipleship. He possesses a passion for connecting people to the church through small groups and loves coaching other churches to do the same. John lives in Warrenton, Virginia with his wife, Melinda and their five children.

JOHN M. MOZINGO

Notes

1.   Mark Zuckerberg, "Building Global Community", February 16,2017, https://www.facebook.com/notes/mark-zuckerberg/building-global-community/10154544292806634/

2.   Cade Metz, "Mark Zuckerberg's Answer to a World Divided by Facebook", February 16, 2017, https://www.wired.com/2017/02/mark-zuckerbergs-answer-world-divided-facebook-facebook/

3.   Perry Noble, "10 Characteristics of a Growing Church", August 28, 2011, https://churchleaders.com/outreach-missions/outreach-missions-how-tos/150777-perry_noble_10_characteristics_of_growing_churches.html

4.   Joel Comiskey, "2000 Years of Small Groups, (Moreno Valley: CCS Publishing, 2015) p. 184.

5.   Andy Stanley, Sermon Series: Simply Irresistible, Part 3: Authentic Community, May 3, 2004, https://vimeo.com/48026219

6.   Reggie Joiner, "Losing Your Marbles: A Lot Can Happen in a Week : Playing for Keeps : What You Do This Week Matters. (Cumming, GA: Orange, a division of the reThink Group, Inc. Hansen, E., & Ivy, K, 2013) p. 201

7.   Andrea Robbins, "The Shocking Truth About How Many Emails Are Sent", March 19, 2018, https://www.campaingmonitor.com/blog/emial-marketing/2018/03/shocking-truth-about-how-many-emails-are-sent/

8.   Aaron Earls, "Culture Change: Recognize the Value of Small Groups. June 5, 2014, https://factsandtrends.net/2014/06/05/culture-change-recognize-the-value-of-small-grodawnups/

9.   Mark Chaves, "National Congregations Study. 2006, http://www.soc.duke.edu/natcong/

10.   Marva Dawn, "A Royal Waste of Time: The Splendor of Worshipping God and Being Church for the World", (Grand Rapids: W.B. Eerdmans Pub., 1999) p. 1.

11.   Matthew Henry, "Psalm 29", https://www.biblestudytools.com/commentaries/matthew-henry-complete/psalms/29.html

Made in USA - North Chelmsford, MA
1239347_9781724801302
02.25.2021 0905